To: Cody

Pleasure to meet & work with you.

2 Levels to heal all Trauma
1 - Physical - Forgive
2 - Spiritual - Thank & Love

All the Best!!   [signature]   *May 20/15*

Slap! Punch! Kick! Mom and Dad Are Home
An Autobiography

GREG L. REID

Copyright © 2013 by Greg L. Reid. All rights reserved.

Published in Canada by Greg L. Reid

First Edition published July 2013

Front cover art by SIGN DESIGN, Custom Graphics Shop Inc., Linden, Alberta, Canada
Cover and internal design © 2013 by Greg L. Reid

No part of this book may be reproduced in any form or by an electronic or mechanical means including information storage and retrieval systems – except in the case of brief quotations embodied in critical articles or reviews – without permission in writing from its author, Greg L. Reid.

This publication is designed to provide accurate and authoritative information in regard to the subject matter covered. It is sold with the understanding that the author / publisher are not engaged in rendering professional health service. If professional health assistance is required, the services of a competent professional person should be sought.

All brand names and product names used in this book are trademarks, registered trademarks, or trade names of their respective holders.

Published by Greg L. Reid with the assistance of DesJardins NuMedia

ISBN-13: 978-0991935208
ISBN-10: 0991935209

DEDICATED TO MY SISTERS

TABLE OF CONTENTS

Preface

Prologue

Misery Loves Company

1	Innisfail	Pg 1
	- My Ultimate Beating	Pg 2
	- Rooster For Dinner	Pg 5
	- Whipped	Pg 7
	- Marj	Pg 12
	- Santa	Pg 14
2	Prince George	Pg 17
	- Bacon	Pg 18
	- And Eggs (Cut me a stick, please)	Pg 22
	- Leaving Prince George	Pg 24
3	Whitelaw	Pg 27
	- Driving Home	Pg 28
	- Eating Bran	Pg 34
	- Allen and the Bees	Pg 37
	- Kelly	Pg 40
	- Picking Berries	Pg 43
	- Maw Puss	Pg 45
	- Marj and the Dogs	Pg 49
	- Bikes and Freedom	Pg 53
	- Locked Out	Pg 54
	- Leaving Whitelaw	Pg 55
4	Red Deer	Pg 59
	- Moving to Red Deer	Pg 60
	- Spinal Damage	Pg 64
	- God and the Church	Pg 68

4	Red Deer ... cont'd	
	- Sweetums	Pg 72
	- Granddad Washes the Dishes	Pg 76
	- Moving Out	Pg 78
	- My First Girlfriend & Leaving Home	Pg 83
	- A Change of Forecast	Pg 85
	- Border Paving – Rick	Pg 87
	- Master of My Abode	Pg 93
	- Changing My Life	Pg 99
	- Martial Arts	Pg 105
	- The Bully	Pg 108
5	Author's Note	Pg 113
6	Sierra	Pg 115
	- Sierra: Excerpt From Book Two	Pg 116

Preface

I have tried to present the information in this book as honestly and accurately as I can, given the amount of time that's passed and all the emotions those memories carry for me. I have spared no details, as you soon will discover.

It isn't impossible that I may have slightly distorted some of the facts from my memory because of the toll that the trauma and pain has taken on me. I am only human, so I ask your forgiveness for whatever discrepancies and mistakes, however small, have slipped into this book. I wrote this to honour the life my sisters and I had during our childhood. I want this to be a record of all the pain and sadness we have lived through, so anyone out there that has lived through similar circumstances might feel less alone.

Writing this has helped me come to terms with what has happened. Today, I no longer feel the weight of all those memories.

The names of my parents are true, other names have been changed.

Prologue

"Greg, I want you to make up a list of the worst of the worst things that have happened to you."

"Greg, are you listening?"

"Yeah", I was listening. My mind was racing, sitting there in a marriage counsellor's office on a sunny, July day in Abbotsford, B.C. 2010. The "worst of the worst list". Is she fucking kidding me? Where do I start and what do I tell her?

"I heard you Bev, I'm just thinking for a minute."

"Go ahead and take your time."

I'm 48 years old, estranged and separated from my wife of 24 years. My three young adult children and I are going through the worst part of our lives, although I thought I had already been through the worst parts of mine.

My past had finally caught up to me. For 48 years, I hadn't thought of my abusive childhood. I had spent my entire life not acknowledging my past; now she wanted me to make a fucking list. I made a deal with my past that we would not talk to each other, well, that was a deal that didn't fucking work out. Bev's hourly rate was $120. This was going to cost me. I had anger issues, marijuana addiction, ever-changing employment, an unhappy wife, and an unhappy life. You need not be an idiot to finally see the signs of a breakdown.

I sighed to myself. I would tell Bev everything. There were so many horrible events, I didn't know if Bev could handle them. I didn't know if I could handle them. I felt clammy and sick to my stomach.

I had a connection with Bev, as my wife and I had been seeing her for marriage counselling for many weeks.

As part of a group discussion with the three of us, it was agreed that Bev and I needed to work on my childhood abuse issues. Work on that first, and then work on the marriage and the relationship with my wife. I trusted Bev, and I didn't trust many people. I was going to do the one thing I had so zealously hung onto not doing my whole life - telling a perfect stranger the worst of the worst. Fuck me.

"So, you want the worst of the worst list. Are you sure you can handle what I tell you?"

"That's what I'm here for Greg."

"Well, if you want it you got it."

"Good. Here's some paper and a pen. Start jotting down the events and we can see what we have to work on in the following sessions. I recommend starting with your first abuse or trauma memories and then work forward in time or by location if you moved a lot, which you did."

"Well the earliest would be just before I started kindergarten, when we lived in Innisfail, Alberta. It's about 20-30 minutes south of Red Deer."

"That's a good start Greg. Can you tell me a bit about the event? Was it physical or sexual abuse?

"No, it was physical."

"And, can you tell me about the event?"

"Yeah, I can tell you about it Bev. I call it my Ultimate Beating."

Misery Loves Company

I have no photos or physical history of my life as a child. One of my only surviving photos is a picture in a high school yearbook. It is as if I never existed.

It amazes me that I know so little about the two people who had the biggest impact on me in my early years. The specific dates I do know are few – I only have a general timeline of my immediate family life, as well as many vivid memories and episodes. My two younger sisters were born, the youngest in 1965, the middle one two years before her. I was born on March 31st, 1962 in Trochu, Alberta. Since there was no hospital in Trochu, I was delivered in a nun's convent infirmary by Dr. Hay. Later, I found out he became a pyromaniac. He was apparently caught setting barns and buildings on fire and was institutionalized.

My mother was nee Marjorie Elisa Ross. She was born on December 23, 1940, in Stettler, Alberta. She has a sister, Helen and a brother, Alex. Her mother, or Granny, as I called her, was Ruby Ross nee Thompson, and her husband was Roy Ross.

I was told Roy's father, Jack Ross, was the Territorial Marshal of the State of Minnesota. I remember my grandfather telling me stories about his dad. His father was a hard-drinking, mean man who could kill a man if it was needed. One of his jobs was to pick up prisoners in small towns awaiting trial, and escort them to court. Every prisoner he was assigned would be hanged if found guilty. Because of his job, he had had to kill a few of the prisoners because they did not want to go to court willingly. His life motto was "kill them before they kill you."

Granny's family disowned her when they found out her plans to marry Roy. They considered him a "bad boy." She met Roy when he and his father came up to Canada for the homesteading. This was a time when the government gave settlers free land in return for "breaking" it, and living on it.

Breaking land, also known as sod-busting, meant turning raw land into fields, ready for growing crops.

Jack and Roy chose the Big Valley area of Alberta. The land was flat and dry with the Red Deer River running through it, the same river that Jack would later drown in.

The land in Big Valley was well suited to raising cattle and horses and Jack enjoyed breaking and training horses. Jack passed on these skills to Roy. There was always a demand for a horse to be broken and trained so Roy was able to make money off the land and through horses. His neighbours would remember him, and say that if Roy could have been as good with people as he was with horses, he would have had a lot more friends. Alas, Roy was a harsh man and a heavy drinker.

Ruby met Roy when her family took their horses to be broken and trained. She began seeing Roy often, even after her family expressed deep disapproval. Though Roy's father spent years raising him to be hard and mean, Ruby thought she could change him to meet her family's expectations. From what I can tell, that change never came. They never shared the same bed from as far back as I can remember. She never called him by his name, referring to him only as the "old fool."

Though I don't know all the details of their family life, there were stories of physical abuse, alcoholism, and even whispers of sexual abuse. They lived in an isolated location, and Ruby didn't have family support. Living in this family meant that Roy abused my mother.

My father was Allen Borden Reid, born in 1932 in Nova Scotia, though the exact city is unknown to me. I don't know his mother's name or her story. I do know of his father, Bill Reid, who married a rich widow for her money.

After having a few kids, he took her entire inheritance and shipped his son, Allen, to live with his brother, Melvin Reid and his wife Ruby, who were rumoured to be cousins.

I also believe Allen had an older sister, though I don't know what happened to her.

Allen's uncle was a rancher and a farmer. His land was directly across the Red Deer River from Roy and Ruby's farm, by the town of Elnora, Alberta. Allen was dumped by his Dad to live with Mel and Ruby when he was in grade six or seven and his education ended there. His new family saw school as a waste of time. Though they didn't want Allen to live with them, they saw he could be useful as a farm hand.

Allen was put to hard work at about twelve years old. Like my mother's father, Mel was a mean drinker, who hit people when he was drunk. I am sure he beat and abused Allen throughout his time at the farm.

My mother was an attractive young woman. Allen was not her first choice, and initially she was not interested in dating him, but Ruby persuaded her. Marj was sexually active at the time, and her mother feared she would get pregnant out of wedlock, so out of pressure, she began dating him. Eventually they became a couple and were married around 1960. I was born two years later. I was told that Marj resented me and the freedom she lost after she found herself tied down with a crying baby. She blamed Ruby for pressuring her into marriage and giving her the grandchild she wanted, so she considered it Ruby's duty to help raise me.

They came to an agreement that I would spend every summer at her farm in Big Valley throughout my school years.

This home was to become my sanctuary and the only source of stability I would have. I probably would have completely lost it if I didn't have that as my escape.

GRANNY'S FARM

I learned many valuable lessons there and made many happy memories. I had freedom, space, safety and responsibilities.

When I was there, someone else was encouraging me to be a better me. At home, I had to be my own teacher in learning to avoid all I did not want to become.

I remember one summer my Granny bought me a yellow Japanese transistor radio. I learned to tune it to catch the music on the waves. It was amazing that I could do that.

The radio helped to show me that there was a huge world out there, a world so different from the one I knew. I would go on to use music, as well as my second discovery at Granny's, reading, to escape the pain at home. Always, too soon, my parents would come for me and bring me home again come last week of August.

I had mixed emotions in the fall – I had to return to my normal life. That meant being around my parents, but it also meant school. I loved school because of the encouragement I received from my teachers for doing well. That too gave me stability, as well as teaching me to have confidence in myself. I had an identity – I had something I was good at. Marj resented me for my success in school. I was a reminder of the life she would never have. She had to live out her fate as the wife of an uneducated, abusive, raging alcoholic.

The marriage between my parents was filled with anger and violence. My mother felt herself cornered into marrying my father. When she had issues with him, there was no one to help her through it. Living in a small farm town made the circumstances especially hopeless. Marriage problems back then were not talked about. The police, neighbours, and the community as a whole generally did not want domestic abuse and family issues to be dealt with out in public. It was supposed to be kept within the household – the main motto was "out of sight, out of mind." Whenever a fight broke out or a noise complaint was called in to the police, they only came to see it stopped and quieted down – they took no further steps to keep the abusive family member from further harming their family.

Marriages between husbands and wives were supposed to withstand alcoholism and abuse. In families such as mine, the marriage was built upon those behaviours. Divorce was considered a serious sin back then – everyone was supposed to just "work it out" on their own. You dealt with your issues on your own and you told no one about it. There was no such thing as counselling in the rural towns, nor were there community resources or social services. The saddest part is that some of the other families in our communities dealt with their issues the same way. It was normal to beat your wife and kids.

It was also hard for anyone to reach out to us from our family, friends or community. We would leave or be forced to leave before people really understood what was happening. I'm sure their general reaction was, "Good riddance." However, when we moved to a city, the police were much stricter and more helpful, and we found the social services to help us. I suppose it's natural for the rural areas to progress slower.

My father worked wherever he could find work. We didn't live in one place for very long – either Allen would notice people getting an idea of what was happening in our home, or he'd run away from the terrible reputations he would gain. Sometimes, his employers would just get sick of his attitude, and he'd get fired.

Allen drank because he was angry. In his defense, there was a lot to be angry about. He was angry over the abuse he lived through in his own childhood. He was angry at being abandoned by his father and at lacking a proper education. He was trapped in working crummy jobs where he'd be breaking his back, working in dangerous conditions, and not making enough money to support his growing family.

At home, he had a wife who thought she married below her. She considered him second choice, and never stopped reminding him of it. They were unfaithful to each other throughout their marriage.

At some point, Allen truly snapped. He became angry, violent, cruel and downright evil. He was a man who felt joy and pleasure by bringing suffering to others.

Allen and Marj had classic co-dependence issues. When Allen would have his outburst of violence, Marj would copy him. It was terrifying to see her horror when she witnessed what he would do, only to mimic her own abuse on us afterwards. This behaviour turned into a kind of reflex for her. I'm not sure why she did this, but in addition to a battered past, I believe she had issues with mental health - she may have been bipolar.

Yet Marj knew abusing us was wrong and acknowledged it. When her frenzy of fury would subside, she would come to her senses and be overcome with remorse and guilt. Unlike Marj, Allen never cleaned up his mess. He never apologized, he never confessed to making a mistake, and he never told us he loved us. My father never told me he loved me. Never. I can't remember him ever expressing compassion, except for a few moments with a family pet. His meanness and anger went far deeper than Marj's – he was cruel to the core.

Both of my parents came from alcoholic, abusive and angry fathers. They both accepted the same fate for their own marriage. Misery loves company – that pretty much sums up the relationship between my parents, and that was the environment in which three children were raised.

The following stories are from my counselling sessions. They are the worst of the worst. There are many other events that happened to us over the years, but the stories presented here were the most traumatic. I relived them during therapy because they had brought the most physical and emotional damage to my sisters and me.

My Granny stories were part of my counselling with Bev, for her to show me someone cared for and loved us kids.

Slap, punch, kick; Mom and Dad are home.

SLAP! PUNCH! KICK! MOM AND DAD ARE HOME

Innisfail

My Ultimate Beating

We moved to Innisfail the year I began kindergarten. Allen and Marj rented a small house on one acre on the south end of town, about a mile away from the school. We left when I was finishing grade two. My two younger sisters were born there. Allen had bought a water tank truck, and was paid to deliver water to rig sites every day. He was gone early in the morning and home late at night.

During my first few weeks at school, I began to realize I had really bad parents. Talking with the other kids and seeing how they played made me realize my family life was different from theirs. I asked the other kids if they got spanked for being bad. Some said yes and others said they were made to sit out or miss out on family activities. I asked some of the other boys if they were beaten by their mom and dad. They all said no, that never happened.

They asked me what the difference between spanking and beating was. I explained that a spanking was just being hit on your ass, but a beating was being slapped, punched, kicked and thrown to the ground. A few of the boys said they had been hit and thrown to the ground but it was only when their dad had gotten really mad, and it only happened once or twice.

One summer evening when I was about five or six or years old, Marj went out and left us under Allen's care. Marj and Allen had had a big fight earlier that day and he had started drinking heavily right after she left. It was close to suppertime and he was in the kitchen making dinner, banging and slamming pots and pans. I could hear him muttering and talking out loud to himself. He was getting angrier and angrier as he drank more and more.

My two sisters were playing with dolls in the living room and I wanted to join them. They said no, since I didn't play fair and would tear the heads off their dolls for fun. As I tried to push my way in they yelled at me to leave them alone.

From the kitchen I heard Allen. "That's enough."

He stomped into the living room and I could tell he was drunk.

"What the fuck is going on here? What are you kids doing?"

He reached out to hit my sisters.

"No it wasn't them, it was me making all the noise." I stepped out in front of them.

He looked at me with his bloodshot eyes, blinking and thinking for a second. He grabbed me and said, "I'm tired of your kids' shit all the time. I'm sick of it."

As he lifted me in the air in front of him, he kicked open the front door. Then, with all his might, he slammed me onto the driveway.

The explosion of pain was something I had never felt before. Both my parents had beaten me before but this pain was way beyond anything I had ever experienced.

The impact knocked the breath out of me. I could not breathe at all, no matter how hard I tried. There were explosions of bright white lights in my head. My whole body felt pain from head to toe. I remember lying there with the front porch light shining around me. I had just drunk some milk before and I puked it up. The blood came from my nose and mouth, mixing with the milk in swirls, and turning the blood to a pink cotton candy colour.

I still couldn't breathe, but when I looked at the milk swirls, they looked so beautiful. I felt a sudden rush in my body and a roaring in my head as I passed out. I couldn't feel pain anymore, but I felt myself being lifted, as if someone was carrying me. There was no one around me. I felt more of the lifting sensation all over my body and I rose up and saw myself from above. I felt a warm sensation come over me and a blinding white and gold light all around. It felt so warm and peaceful. I was surrounded by light. I didn't feel scared at all. I felt very happy. All the pain I felt moments ago was now gone, everything felt better. I heard a woman's voice coming from the light. The voice told me that I couldn't go with the light like I wanted to. I didn't want to listen. I knew this place was better than where I was.

I didn't want to stay with my family.

The woman's voice told me I had to stay where I was - it wasn't my time yet. The voice told me the pain in my life was not over, that I would feel more pain in the years to come, but it was okay. "They" would be there to help me through it. I was told I had some important things to do in life, and I needed to stay here with this family. I felt myself yelling that I didn't want to stay! I wanted to go with her.

She told me I had to remember that I was not allowed to take my own life to come back to this place. She told me that one day, I would have this experience again, but not for a long time. I didn't understand what was happening to me.

I began to feel heavy and slow and the voice became quieter and quieter. The white and gold light began to fade and the warmth was being taken over by coldness. I saw myself from above again but I seemed to be falling down and forward towards my body sprawled out on the driveway. I had a sense of falling again, but not in the way I was thrown to the ground by my father. It was a kind of rushing, swirling feeling.

I suddenly could feel the air on my face as I took a ragged breath in. My body was on fire from pain. I threw up and convulsed on the ground. I laid there for what seemed to be hours unable to move or call out. My father did not, even once, come out to see if I was okay.

I wondered if I had dreamt this or imagined it. I knew something had happened to me, since I could feel cold air and the very real pain in my body. After what seemed hours, I saw headlights turn into the driveway. I felt terrible fear as I thought the car wouldn't see me and drive over me. The car stopped and the door opened. Marj jumped out and ran to me, crying when she saw me. She picked me up in her arms and ran into the house.

She met Allen inside the house. "What the fuck are you doing? I go out and leave you with the kids and you try to kill your son. What the hell is the matter with you?" She screamed as she pushed by him.

She took me to the bathroom and cleaned me up. The whole house was a golden color and there were rainbow coloured ribbons everywhere. I heard strange noises coming from everywhere, but especially from above. I spent the rest of the night and the next few days throwing up and feeling dizzy and out of sorts. Strange buzzing sounds went through my head and my body hurt from top to bottom. I have never felt this much pain in my life, up to present day. I also will never fear death again. I know that death will be an old friend to me one day, and I will welcome it.

Rooster For Dinner

Later that summer, my sisters and I spent time at Granny's farm. One day it was very hot, as it often was there. I believe heat leads idle minds to trouble, as it did that day.

My sisters and I were hanging around the chicken pens. My youngest sister was about two or three at the time. She had been chasing the fat old hens. We ran them back and forth between us, upsetting them and working them into a state. We all thought this was a grand game, but eventually my middle sister and I went off to get into some other mischief, leaving our youngest sister to play near the chickens. My middle sister and I were a short distance away when we heard our youngest sister screaming. We ran around the henhouse towards her.

There in front of us was a big, white, tough Leghorn rooster, just like the one from Bugs Bunny. It was sitting on top of my little sister, pecking at her head. The rooster was pulling out tufts of hair as my sister and I watched in disbelief. We'd never seen Granny's rooster attack a person before. My little sister was rolling around and screaming her head off like she was being killed. My sister and I ran towards Granny's house, yelling for her to come out. The three of us must have been awfully loud.

We met Granny coming out of the house. "What the hell is going on with you kids?"

We both started talking and yelling at the same time. Granny looked past us towards our little sister. She took ten long quick strides and soon had the rooster by the neck in a death grip. The rooster flapped its wings and tried to break free while she pulled an axe out of a nearby chopping block.

She looked straight at me. "Come and help me."

The rooster was putting up such a terrible fight that she had to drop the axe and use both hands to hold him. I picked up the axe and followed Granny, who was holding the flapping, squawking rooster, around the corner of the henhouse to the other chopping block.

This chopping block had nails on it, bent into the shape of a hoop. We all knew that this was where chickens met their death. The hoop let you put in the chicken's head and pull the neck really long so you could make a clean chop with the axe. This was the infamous, custom-made chicken guillotine.

Granny put the rooster's neck into the hoop as she took the axe from my hand. Without any ceremony or hesitation, she lopped off its head. I will never forget that scene. The axe was buried deep in the chopping block. Blood spurted from the bird's headless body as its limbs continued to flap. Granny made the three of us help her pluck off its feathers so we could prepare him for dinner. We were very quiet and polite at the dinner table that night.

After that, we stopped chasing the fat old hens.

Whipped

One weekend, Allen and Marj decided to take us camping. It was a hot, dry summer so we all thought it would be a good idea.

Allen and Marj spent the whole week gathering necessary supplies: tent, sleeping bags, cooking stove, food and Allen's large supply of beer and hard liquor. When Friday came around, we loaded up the truck and headed out. As soon as Allen put the truck into gear, he opened the first of many beers. Marj started complaining about the drinking and driving, so fighting began a block from the house. We knew it was not going to be a good time. My sisters and I wanted to turn around and go home. At least we had places to hide there.

By the time we arrived at our campsite, Allen had developed into a full rage. He threw everything from the truck onto the ground, and then put all his precious beer in the stream next to our campsite to keep it cool. Then, his back to us, he sat on a rock by the stream, opened another beer and continued drinking.

Marj and I put up the tent and the girls unpacked all the food and supplies. Then the girls and I decided to explore along the stream. We were gone for about an hour when we started getting hungry. We started back, hoping to find dinner cooking, but heard instead the sound of fighting.

There was the sound of someone being slapped, followed by Marj's crying. When we got to the site, Marj sat there in tears, looking very angry, while Allen was back at the stream opening another beer. I asked Marj if everything was okay, but she didn't answer.

"We're hungry, could we have something to eat?" I asked.

She said nothing, so I repeated myself, louder this time. She quickly turned towards me and glared.

"Is that all you ever want, food?" she snapped. "I'm fucking sick and tired of always waiting on you. If it isn't one thing it's another, aren't you ever fucking satisfied? I'll make dinner when I'm good and ready, or maybe I won't make dinner at all. Ask your fucking dad to do it."

I knew not to engage Marj after she and Allen fought, but we hadn't eaten since morning. It was obvious that Allen wouldn't be making dinner since he was getting drunker and drunker. I knew it was dangerous to push her when she was like this, but my hunger was too strong.

I walked over to where the food was kept and started going though the supplies. I didn't notice the dishes piled on the cooler and accidentally knocked them over. Some of the glasses fell to the ground and broke.

When Marj heard this she turned around and screamed, "What the fuck are you doing, you stupid kid, I told you to leave it alone!"

As I bent down to pick up the glass, I heard her coming towards me. She grabbed me from behind and threw me to the ground. When I fell, she grabbed my pants and underwear and pulled them down.

As I struggled to get away from her, I saw she had some sort of whip in her hand. I think it was the truck's radio antenna. She made a slash across my exposed backside. All along the lash, pain flared like fire. She began screaming at me as she whipped me along my back and my ass. The girls heard my screaming and ran to hide in a nearby bush.

I crawled on the ground as I tried to get away. The pain from each lash didn't subside. She whipped me until my whole body was on fire. It just went on and on. I remember protecting my face and the front of my body by crawling on my belly as I tried to move away. I cried and screamed for her to stop. I could see blood coming from my lower back where the skin had been cut open.

I finally crawled alongside our pick-up truck and slid underneath. I was covered in urine from peeing myself after the first slashes. As I put my hand on my lower back, I could feel it slick with blood, the dirt mixed in with it.

Marj was standing by the truck, her face a mask of pure fury. She was screaming at me to come out. She couldn't reach me and tried to poke me with a stick she found nearby. Every time the stick came near, I rolled out of the way. She finally stormed off. I lay there curled up in a ball, crying, my cuts still bleeding. I finally passed out from the pain.

I don't know how long I was out, but I remember being grabbed and pulled out by both my parents. Marj was crying and saying how sorry she was for hurting me. She said she really loved me and everything would be okay. I could barely move. Allen, though drunk, looked horrified by my condition.

They took me down to the stream and washed me off. The water was freezing but the cold helped soothe the pain. The two of them cleaned me up and put bandages on my slashes.

"Everything will be okay," they repeated.

They had made dinner and brought me to the table so I could eat. My sisters had been crying, frightened by my condition. I stared at my food, numb.

"Come on Greg, have something to eat, it will make you feel better," said Marj.

I didn't move so Marj picked up some of the food and started feeding it to me by hand. The burning sensation in my body grew stronger and stronger. I started crying again. Marj held me gently and said it would be all right and that she loved me. I wished she would stop saying that.

I finished a bit of my dinner and went to lie down. Marj had made up my sleeping bag and she helped me and tucked me in. I fell into a fitful sleep.

The next morning, my back felt like it was on fire every time I moved as scabs had started to form. Yet there were no plans to take me to a hospital.

Later that day, as my middle sister was walking to the stream, Marj yelled for her to bring back some water. When she said that, she threw a pot for the water at her. I sat on the bench watching the pot spin crazily in the air. The handle made it wobble. As my sister tried to grab it, the handle struck her hand, and the pot bounced up her arm. It bounced funny and the edge hit her on the head, causing her scalp to split open. I sat there in horror as her head started to bleed.

Marj quickly ran to her, "I didn't mean it, it was an accident!"

Marj grabbed her and took her to the truck to look for bandages but they were gone. Everything was used on my slashes. Marj threw her in the truck and took her to the nearest town to get stitches, leaving my youngest sister and me with Allen.

As she left, Marj yelled at Allen to take everything down and have it packed up when she got back. Allen started packing up. My little sister and I just sat there. Everything was packed up by the time my sister, with new stitches on her scalp, returned from the hospital. Allen and Marj put everything in the truck and we drove away.

I remember this event again and again and again. When people see the scars on my back, some ask how I got them. I tell them I was whipped when I was a kid.

* * *

Many years later, I was working in road construction, visiting Oakland, California for an asphalt trade show. There were about eight to ten black guys sitting around drinking beer and bitching about white people and their oppression of the black man. I think they were talking like this for my benefit, since I was a pasty white Canadian visitor. I remember one guy going on about how he was "whipped" every day by his piece-of-shit boss. As I sat there listening, I got angry.

Finally I said, "Any of you fuckers ever been whipped?"

Some of the guys just sat there blankly staring at me, not sure of what they'd just heard.

I said it again, louder this time. "Any of you fuckers ever been whipped before?"

No one said anything.

"I have." I pulled up my shirt to show them the scars on my back. They all stopped talking and stared at me.

"You think only black people get whipped? White people learned to be experts in whipping by practicing on other white people first."

I stood there for a minute with my shirt pulled up. Then I walked away. No one said a word.

The next day, I went back to the trade show. All the black people there must have heard about my outburst because they treated me completely different. They all said hi to me and introduced themselves. Many asked if I wanted a beer or something to eat. Could they get me anything?

I could see they still had a problem with some of the other white guys at the show, but not with me. I was treated graciously all day. A couple of the guys even drove me to the airport the next day so I wouldn't have to take a cab.

I think I learned something from that. People who have suffered or feel like the underdog connect with each other. They want to show their support, no matter how small the gesture.

Marj

Over time my parents had become part of a group that was wild and partied all the time. Every day, the group would drink, either at our home or one of the group's. Allen was drunk or drinking all the time. Men were always at our place, sometimes with Allen, sometimes without. Marj brought men over to the house; they were referred to as "uncles" or good friends of the family. Funny, because for being relatives or good friends of the family, I never remembered who they were.

Sometimes, only one man would visit while Allen was away. They would go into her bedroom and lock the door, staying there for hours. Sometimes if we knocked on the door wanting something, Marj would make us go outside and "play," locking the doors behind us. She would say she would let us in in awhile.

One evening in summer, late at night, Marj had one of her male friends over. Allen was out of town. My sisters and I were in bed and Marj and her friend were in the living room talking. After a while, I woke up to the sound of my mother's voice. She was upset with the man and yelling at him, "Stop it. No."

My bedroom was at the back of the house and I heard her struggling to fight him off. I heard the sound of cloth being ripped. The man was getting mad and his voice rose. Again, I heard the sound of cloth ripping and Marj getting more upset. It sounded just like my parents fighting except it wasn't Allen she was fighting with.

Marj yelled, "Get out!"

I could hear her crying as she ran past my bedroom. She opened the back door as the man yelled after her. His footsteps boomed through the house as he followed her. He opened the back door and chased her. I was scared. I left my room and came outside to help her.

We had a raised wooden deck in the backyard. I had put plywood and some boards around the platform at ground level and turned it into a play fort. It was built for a little kid, but Marj had managed to squeeze inside it. The man reached in with his hands to try and pull her out. Her clothes were ripped apart.

I ran to the man and yelled, "Stop hurting my mom!"

As I slapped, punched and kicked him, he turned to me, grabbed my neck and shoulders and threw me away from him. I flew through the air and landed, the wind knocked out of me. I couldn't get up. I heard him grab Marj and pull her out from the fort. She cried as he raped her a few yards away from where I was. I could hear everything he did to her and I could do nothing but lie there and cry. After he finished, he got up, pulled up his pants, and walked off to his truck in the driveway. He got in and drove away.

When Allen returned to Innisfail, he was told of the rape. He was sure he knew who had done it. Later, I would find out it was a drinking buddy they both knew. One night, I was riding with Allen in his water truck. He saw a pick-up truck coming down the road towards us. He sped up and moved into the middle of the road, forcing the other truck to turn. It swerved and drove into the ditch.

He kept a grease gun under the passenger seat in case the truck or equipment needed lubrication. He stopped the truck and grabbed it before getting out. Allen ran towards the ditch and pulled open the driver's door, yanking the man out. Then he punched him and knocked him onto the ground. I watched everything, frozen with fear, under the headlight of our truck.

I watched Allen beat the man about his head and body with the grease gun. I could see blood spurting from where he was hit. Allen screamed at him, shouting he was going to kill him for what he had done. Allen hit him again and again until the man stopped holding up his hands to defend himself. He fell to the ground and stopped moving, but Allen continued to hit him. There was blood all over the man's body, head and face. He looked dead. I was crying as Allen got into the truck and left him dead, dying or near it, in that ditch by the lonely country road.

As I got older and received counselling on these two incidents, I connected the attack with Marj's rape. I used to think it was my fault that I couldn't help Marj, but through therapy, I learned to accept that I was a little boy, and there was nothing I could have done. It was not my fault.

Santa

After Marj's sexual assault, constant beatings for all of us, and never ending police visits, Marj made up her mind. She left Allen, taking us with her. We stayed in the same town, though.

We were sent to the welfare office and given government housing to live in. We got a tiny, four-room house. It had two bedrooms, a kitchen and a living area at the doorway. Our bathroom was very small and had no tub or shower in it, only the sink and the toilet. This was to be our new home.

We moved into the house in late fall. We would be spending our Christmas there. The town was very small itself and everyone knew each other's business. Naturally, the stories of the Reids' antics spread like wildfire. Most parents didn't let their kids play with us. We were sad and lonely. We had to listen to stories about our parents retold by the other kids at school. It was horrible there. The kids would jeer at us daily and call us the 'welfare kids'.

Allen found out where we lived. He would drive his water truck by our neighbourhood and honk his horn. It was weird, even for us kids.

That Christmas, the welfare people came by with a box of food and Christmas presents. I knew we needed food; there wasn't much in the house. Marj wouldn't take anything at first, out of pride. She didn't want to show people that she needed charity. But with some gentle urging from the social workers, she finally broke down and accepted the food and toys. I remember the face and eyes of the man who was dropping them off. He was a big man with white hair and piercing blue eyes. I had never seen eyes that colour before.

Later that day, Santa was supposed to meet all the kids at the town centre. The whole town went down to see him and we did, too.

There was a sleigh and horses around him, and we discovered, to our great surprise, that all the kids would receive a gift. My sisters and I eagerly lined up to meet him and get our toy. For the first time in a long time, the kids in the line up were treating us like normal kids. There was no name calling or pushing and shoving. I felt like an ordinary kid meeting Santa like everyone else.

My two sisters were ahead of me to meet Santa. As they sat on his knee and told him what they wanted for Christmas, I looked closer at him. He wore big black boots and a bright red Santa jacket. He had a big, white, flowing beard, spectacles, and a Santa cap, like any good Santa should. But what stood out the most about him were his piercing blue eyes - eyes I had seen a few hours ago when he dropped off our food and toys. When it was my turn, our eyes met and we both knew instantly that we had met earlier in the day.

We just stared at each other for a few seconds and he broke the silence by saying, "Here you go little boy, look what Santa brought you."

He handed me one of the better gifts in his bag and wished me a merry Christmas. I didn't even sit on his knee and tell him what I wanted. We both knew he wasn't Santa. Even with Santa, our secrets weren't safe.

There is a song by Everclear called "*I Will Buy You a New Life*". The lyrics go:

> *I hate those people who love to tell you*
>
> *'Money is the root of all that kills'*
>
> *They have never been poor, no, they've never known*
>
> *The joy of a welfare Christmas*

I have.

Prince George

Bacon

As always, Allen and Marj got back together and eventually the community ran our family out of Innisfail, so we moved to Prince George, BC.

OUR HOUSE IN PRINCE GEORGE, BC

Here, Allen decided he was going to work as a lumberjack.

I started grade two at an elementary school down the street, close enough to walk to and from every day. Allen was in the forest cutting down trees for weeks on end. With Allen mostly away, we lived a peaceful life.

One day, Marj left with the girls for a trip back to Alberta. I was left in the care of Allen until they got back, since he was off work for a couple of weeks. I believe Marj thought there was not much Allen could do to me. She had everything set up with the neighbours and I was in school most of the day.

One day, Allen got it in his head that he had to cure his own bacon. Later on, I was told he and his drinking friends discussed it together and decided that curing bacon would be easy and 'something different' to do.

So, Allen set up a smoker and bought some raw uncured pork belly, the first ingredient needed for making bacon. Allen began the smoking and curing process, drinking as he went. After a few days, he considered that enough time had passed for it to be cured. He pulled it out of the smoker and wanted to give it a try. After smelling it, he thought it seemed a bit "off." He waited until I got home from school, at which point he cooked it and fed it to me. He didn't have any himself. It was better to wait and see what would happen with me.

In a few hours, I got violently ill. I threw up on the floor and Allen got angry with me, so he picked me up, threw me into my room and shut the door. He didn't want me vomiting anywhere else in the house.

"You can get sick in there and live with it," he said. "You better knock it off if you want to come out."

I felt terrible. I started to cry and scream from stomach pains. Some of the kids from the neighbourhood came over and asked if I could play. I heard Allen telling them I was sick and wasn't able to, but the kids had heard my screams and got worried. They ran home and told their parents. Some of their moms came over and asked if they could help. Allen said he could take care of me himself; he'd prefer they left us alone.

The women knew Marj and the girls were gone for a few days, and I'm sure red flags were raised when he said that. They could hear me throwing up and asking to come out of the bedroom. Ignoring Allen, the moms pushed their way past him and unlocked my bedroom door. They were hit with the reeking smell of my vomit.

Some of the dads had come over at this point, having found out from their wives that something bad was happening to me. They asked Allen what had happened. The dads told Allen that sending me to the hospital was necessary, though none were aware that the bacon was what had poisoned me. I believe Allen was worried he would get into trouble for what he had done to me. Marj was not there to help, as she usually was whenever he did something stupid or dangerous.

To this day, I thank those moms, whoever they were, for calling the ambulance.

I remember the ambulance staff picking me up and putting me on a bed with wheels. I blacked out as I heard the siren go on. My last thought was that going for a ride in an ambulance was neat.

I don't remember much of my first moments waking up in the hospital. I saw bright lights shining in my eyes and people talking around me. Later in my life, I found out through family that Allen was unwilling to tell the doctors about the bacon. They asked him to give all the details about what I'd eaten so they could determine the cause for the poisoning and begin administering the right treatment. Because the cause of the poisoning was unknown, the doctors had no choice but to perform a spinal tap.

I remember vividly the moment the doctor came into my hospital room and told me they were going to put a needle in my spine to collect fluid, which would show them the cause of the food poisoning. I did not understand what he was saying, but I knew that whatever was coming, it wasn't good.

I was awake when they did the spinal tap. I couldn't receive any drugs, since they would mask the poison in my body. As the doctor told me this, the room quickly filled up with nurses. They all looked very serious. I started to cry. There was no family with me to reassure me.

The nurses quickly lined up on both sides of my bed. I turned to the doctor and watched him take out a long, very large needle. He nodded to the rest of the hospital staff. He told me the spinal tap would be painful, but told me not to move or thrash around or I might become paralyzed. The others quickly grabbed me and rolled me onto my face. They all grabbed a part of me, legs, arms, body, and head. I started to cry and scream and thrash around as I tried to break free of them, but the more I struggled, the tighter they held me down. The doctor was about to begin the process.

As the staff strengthened their hold on me, one of the people holding my head did not realize I couldn't breathe. My head was stuffed right into the pillow. I heard the doctor tell them to hold me tight, as he was about to begin, and this was the critical moment.

I could feel everyone pushing me down harder, and now I couldn't breathe at all. They were starting to suffocate me, which made me struggle even more. I still remember the searing pain when the needle broke my skin and was pushed up into my spine. My entire body felt like it was on fire. Pain was everywhere at once. As I lay there, unable to breathe, I had one thought as I passed out: everybody wants to hurt or kill me. Even perfect strangers.

As I went limp, I think the people holding me down finally realized they were suffocating me.

When I woke up, there was a needle in my arm. A long tube went up, connected to some clear bags that hung from a pole. A nurse was beside me. I reached for the needle but she grabbed my hand and told me not to touch it or pull it out.

"The needle in your arm is giving you medicine to make you feel better," she explained.

I was very tired from all the struggling.

"I'll stay with you until you fall back asleep. You need your rest to get better."

Allen stood outside my hospital room, looking at me. The hospital staff were pissed off at him and would not let him into my room.

For the next few days I just slept, woke up, and fell back to sleep. I was very hungry but the staff would not feed me. When I asked, they told me the needle in my arm fed me medicine, and food was coming from the bags hanging on the poles.

After a few days, Marj and my sisters came to the hospital to visit. Marj cried as she talked to me. She told me she loved me and everything would be okay. Allen didn't come by to see me again.

I was in the hospital for a couple of weeks. The doctor told Marj that if I had been brought to the hospital later, there wouldn't have been anything they could have done for me. The doctor was angry with Allen. He told Marj that if I had been brought in sooner, they could have helped me faster. Allen made them lose precious time by not telling them what he had fed me. The spinal tap could have been avoided altogether if they'd known the cause.

"You are lucky your little boy is still alive," the doctor said.

And Eggs (Cut me a stick, please)

One day, when I was seven or eight, the temperature on Granny's farm reached over 40 degrees Celsius. There seemed to be a connection between stifling heat and the mischief I got into on her farm. I decided it would be a good idea to raid the henhouse and collect all the eggs. You could usually rely on getting around a dozen eggs each time.

After stealing the eggs, I decided to throw them at the pigs. The pigs would get sunburnt in this weather, so they would always dig themselves into the dirt or find shade. I managed to rouse five or six grumpy pigs. They squealed a lot but I didn't care. I began pelting them with eggs. When the eggs hit, they would explode and glue itself to their skin because of the heat. After using up my egg ammo, I went in search of something else to amuse me.

As the day passed, I went about my business, the egged pigs completely forgotten. As always, I had tea in the afternoon with Granny.

As she set up the teapot and cups, she casually asked me for a favour. Always eager to help, I happily agreed.

"Well," she said, "I need a stick yay long." To show me the length, she straightened her arm out, and had me measure from her longest finger to her elbow.

"It needs to be about this thick." Again she made me complete the measurement so I would know exactly what she needed.

"I want the stick smooth, so cut all the twigs and sharp bumps off."

Granny was always fixing things around the farm because granddad never did anything but sit and smoke rolled cigarettes all day, and I liked helping her.

She wanted the stick ready by the time her stories were over, and I scurried off to complete my task. I spent the next hour cutting a stick from a tree to the length and thickness Granny wanted. For the next half hour, I whittled off the bark and twigs and any sharp bumps. When the stick was finished, it was nice and smooth; you could easily run your hand along it. I knew her stories were about to end so I brought the stick back to the house. I handed it to Granny, proud of myself for getting it done in time.

"That's perfect, Greg, exactly what I need. My stories are over, so help me clear away the tea cups and pot, and we'll get to that stick."

I helped carry the cups and plates to the kitchen and put everything away. As we went back out to the living room where she'd left the stick, she grabbed me by the arm, and sat herself down on her chair. She pulled me over her knee, grabbed the stick and proceeded to spank me with it. The shock of being spanked by Granny was more powerful than the actual pain.

"I don't ever want to see you doing that to the pigs or any animals again. Chasing the pigs in this heat could kill them."

She let me go and I ran out of the house sobbing. I was deeply hurt because I knew I deserved the spanking. It must have been hard on Granny to do that. She knew and hated the beatings I had received over the years from my parents. All the same, I needed to have discipline and rules. I was still a child.

Leaving Prince George

Prince George was a short-lived time for us as a family. Allen was always away in the forest-playing lumberjack, and Marj had her usual affairs when he was away.

One day, Marj had a breakdown. She stayed in her bed for days and days, unable to function. I was worried, all of us were. Even Allen was concerned for her health, and that was out of character for him. I think he was mostly terrified of dealing with three small kids on his own. He couldn't cook or clean and he had no idea what to do with us.

After Marj got better and returned to her 'normal' self, we seemed to coast along as a family. My sisters and I had our usual beatings but they weren't as bad as what was to come.

When Allen began working as a lumberjack, the experienced men told him the rules for what to do, but he didn't really listen. He'd let it go in one ear and out the other, thinking he knew best. I guess he thought most of the stuff was common sense. He also probably drank on the job.

One day, one of the trees fell on him. He didn't die, but he did break some of his ribs. After he healed, he decided to put that career behind him, which was probably smart.

Allen decided to make northern Alberta his new home; around the Peace River area. He and Marj had family there. They decided it would be a good change for us. None of us, not even Allen, would expect this next stage in our lives to be the most dramatic and the most violent. We packed up the truck, as we'd done so many times before, and drove away.

GREG L. REID

Whitelaw

Driving Home

One summer day, Allen told me to come with him to run some errands. I was about 8 or 9 years old. Marj had left with the girls for the day. They were at a friend's house, where the girls could play with their friends and Marj and the parents chatted together. It was a girl's thing, so I was left home with the old man.

OUR HOUSE IN WHITELAW, ALBERTA

"Get in the truck, we're going out for a bit," said Allen.

I knew that Allen would stop at the bar for 'one' drink with his friends. He would give me money to buy candy and whatever I wanted, while he was in the bar.

There was a hotel and bar in Whitelaw when we first moved there, but it had mysteriously burned down one winter day. There was a quiet rumour about town about what had happened. Every male of drinking age lived in the bar, and the story went that one day, some of the wives got so sick and tired of having their drunk, abusive husbands coming home every day from the bar, that they simply burnt it to the ground.

The nearest bar was now in Blue Sky, a town 20 minutes north of Whitelaw. Allen was one of the bar's best customers. He would show up at opening time and stay until closing, which was about midnight.

Already anticipating what was to come, I got in the truck, and we were off towards Blue Sky to meet some of his friends. Allen parked the truck in front of the bar and gave me a couple of dollars to buy something at the town's general store. I knew I was going to be in this town for hours and hours.

After Allen went into the bar, I headed towards the general store.

The owner knew all the kids whose dads came to drink. He kept an eye on us, and would suggest we eat better food throughout the day besides candy.

The owner and his wife would let us use their bathroom, and give us water so we would not go thirsty. We all played at the school playground together waiting for our dads to leave the bar. We knew that when one dad left, the others would follow shortly, all except for Allen, who would stay until the bar closed, hours after everyone had left. I would buy comic books to read and join in with the other kids playing tag and hide-and-seek. I liked the swings and play structure too. We would watch the sun set - another day had passed us by. The days were long in northern Alberta, the sun in the summer didn't set until ten or eleven o'clock.

On this day Allen came staggering out of the bar, piss-drunk, unable to stand, with the bar owner helping him into the truck.

He told Allen, "You're too drunk to drive home."

Then he looked at me standing there and said, "Allen, get your kid to drive you home, I'll start it for you and put the truck in the right direction so your kid can do it.'

"Hey, sport," he said to me, "You can do this, right? It's easy, sport, I'll start the truck and point it in the right direction and you can drive your old man home."

I was scared, even though it wasn't dark yet. At least I could see the landscape around me.

"Well sport, you got two choices, you can drive or you can sit here in this truck until morning when your old man sobers up, your choice. Driving is easy. Just go slow and use the brake when you want to slow down or stop. I'll show you and then you're on your own."

I slowly nodded my head up and down while frantic thoughts went through my head. I don't know how to drive, what if I drove into a ditch? What if I hit another car or a car hit us? I was not supposed to drive because I was too young, but I didn't want to spend the night here. I nodded to the bar owner and said I would drive.

"That's the ticket, sport," he said. "Let's get you going then."

He started the truck and backed it out of the parking stall. After he set the truck to park, he jumped out and let me climb in behind the steering wheel.

Again he said, "It's easy sport, just go really slow, it's like riding a bike - you can ride a bike, can't you?"

I nodded and he smiled. "Great, the truck is like a bike. Turn the wheel in the direction you want to go and turn it back straight after you made your turn. See this lever," he said, pointing to the gearshift. "See the different letters on the steering wheel?"

I nodded.

"Good. Each letter means something, D means drive forward, R means reverse, you know, go backwards, and P means park, for when you stop and get out.

All you have to do is line up the red line with the right letter and it will do whatever you want it to. So, when you get home, push the brake down until the truck stops and when it does, push this lever up until the red line aligns with the letter P. Then you just turn the truck off. The rest you don't need to know, like the N function and the 1 and 2 functions. Easy as pie. You know where you live, don't you, sport?"

I nodded.

"Great! Well then off you go," he said as he waved goodbye and walked back into his bar to close up for the night.

I pulled the lever down until the red line aligned with the letter D and started down the road home. I didn't use the gas pedal, as the truck was going fast enough on its own. The speed was the same as when I pedalled my bike – slow for a truck but fast enough for someone with my experience.

I turned onto the highway, my father snoring drunkenly beside me. There was no traffic on the road at this time and I had the whole highway to myself. It took twenty minutes to drive between Blue Sky and Whitelaw, but at my pace it would take an hour.

About fifteen to twenty minutes into my drive, a set of headlights came up behind me. I knew I was driving slow for the highway speed so I switched the car into the shoulder lane and continued driving so the other car would pass me. The headlights didn't pass me though; it followed me for a distance, then a car pulled up beside me.

I looked over and saw an RCMP police car with two policemen. The cop on the passenger side rolled his window down, shining his flashlight on me. The light blinded me. I couldn't see who they were and I almost drove into the ditch before pulling the truck straight again.

Seeing this, the cop turned off his flashlight. He waved at me to stop the truck, so I did what the bar owner had shown me. I pushed on the brake until the truck came to a stop and pulled the lever up until the red line aligned with the letter P. The police car turned on its red and blue lights on the roof and stopped beside me.

As the police car's passenger door opened, the cop said to his partner, "It's a little kid driving the truck."

When the cop stepped out of the car, I could see him putting his hat on and adjusting his belt with his gun on it. I was really, really scared now. I reached over and pushed Allen to wake him up but he was passed out cold. The cop came to my door and opened it. He looked down at me and snapped his flashlight on, shining it at Allen who was snoring loudly.

"What the hell is going on here?" the cop said to me.

I was petrified and said nothing.

"Son," he said gentler to me, "What are you doing driving down the road?"

The other officer got out of the car and went over to Allen. He opened the door and caught him as he fell over.

He shook him and said, "Buddy, Buddy, wake up."

Allen snored loudly. The cop started laughing. "Man, this guy is fucked up. I can't even wake him."

"Hey buddy, had a few too many drinks tonight?" He chuckled to himself.

"Son, where do you live?"

I swallowed nervously. "We live in Whitelaw. I was driving us home because my Dad can't drive and I wanted to go home."

The other cop closed Allen's door and walked over to stand beside his partner.

"Well, what do you think we should do with the pair of them?" he asked.

"There is no way this kid's old man can drive. He is passed out cold and even I can't wake him up," the other one replied.

"Son, can you drive home the rest of the way?" I nodded and quietly said yes.

The other cop said, "We followed this kid for a while and he seemed to be a pretty good driver, slow and safe and he's not too far from home."

Turning to me, he said, "Look son, we have to go to Fairview which is in the opposite direction. We don't want to drive you and your old man home nor do we want to follow you home, we just don't have the time. Are you okay to drive the rest of the way on your own?"

I nodded to him and the cop took one last look at Allen and said, "Well, of the two of them, the kid is obviously the better driver to have on the road. There is no traffic on the highway so it should be clear sailing for you. We will follow you for a bit before we head to Fairview."

The cops climbed back into their police car and waited for me to pull out onto the highway. The truck had been running this whole time, so I pulled the gear down to 'D', and continued on home with the police car following behind us, their police lights flashing. I continued driving at the same speed I was going at, with the cops following me. As I came up to a wider part of the highway, the cops turned off their lights, tooted their horn and did a u-turn. They sped off in the other direction, leaving me to finish the journey on my own.

I pulled into our driveway, pushed on the brake until the truck stopped, pulled the lever up to the letter P, and turned the engine off.

Everyone in the house was sleeping. Since no one could help me bring Allen into the house, I left him there snoring, leaning against the passenger door. I went into the house, climbed into bed and went to sleep.

Eating Bran

I was in the feed shed one day on Granny's farm when I found a big bag of animal-quality bran. So I took a taste. The bran was sweet and I started to eat it by handfuls. After eating my fill, I felt very thirsty so I went to the house to get water. I drank a couple of glasses and went back outside.

Fifteen minutes passed and my stomach began churning. Suddenly, I felt like I had to go to the bathroom so I headed towards the outhouse. Every step I took, the need to go to became stronger and stronger. I sped up and just managed to get in at the last second to pull down my pants. I was sweating like crazy and it seemed like the shit was just never going to stop. I sat in the outhouse as wave after wave went through me.

I finally managed to walk up to Granny's house when the feeling came back again. I turned and ran back, but this time, didn't make it. Still, I kept running, butt cheeks clenched together, trying to hold it back. I sat back down and it started again. I knew I had done something bad to myself.

I tried a third time to head back to the house, minus the soiled underwear. I didn't say anything to her when I passed by. I just collected some water so I could wash my underwear outside.

I went upstairs to find clean clothes, but when I came back to the main level, the feeling swept over me again, and again I made a dash for the outhouse.

Again, I didn't make it. It just seemed to come out on its own, no matter how hard I tried to hold it back. Again, I soiled my bottoms and now, my shit was becoming more liquefied. After this cycle ended, I was down two pairs of underwear and a pair of pants.

I cleaned up as best I could and headed back to the house to get more clean clothes. I rinsed my underwear and pants in the river and hung them on the wire fence to dry.

As I walked back to the house, it happened again. This time, I didn't even bother hiding my soiled pants.

I approached Granny, who was watching her stories.

"Granny, there's something wrong with me. I can't stop going to the bathroom and I messed my underwear and both my pants."

"What have you been eating?"

"Nothing," I said, forgetting about the animal bran I had scarfed down. While Granny and I were talking, another wave came over me and I shit myself again. I felt wretched.

"What did you eat today?" She repeated.

I suddenly remembered the bran.

"What? How much did you eat?" I could tell she was concerned.

"Not very much," I replied.

She grabbed me by the arm and marched me out to the feed shed. "What did you eat in here?"

I knew something was wrong because Granny was talking to me very seriously. I meekly pointed to the big bag of bran she had bought the other day from town for the pigs.

She looked at me sharply. "This is important. Tell me how much you ate."

I started to say that I ate only a little when the wave came over me again and I shit myself just standing there.

I told her, " A couple of handfuls."

"You now know, this is not for people. It's for animals that have problems going to the bathroom. You are not to eat this stuff!"

We went back to the house and she made me stay outside while she called the doctor in Stettler.

She came back outside. "The doctor said you're going to have the runs for at least three or four days, if not longer."

I nodded blankly.

"You have to drink lots of water because it will help flush the bran and everything else through you. Plus, you are losing a lot of water and will become dehydrated otherwise."

"What does 'dehydrated' mean?"

"When you go to the bathroom a lot and have the runs, it takes a lot of the water out of you and you can get really sick. The water loss will hurt your internal organs."

I wailed, "Granny, am I going to die?"

She laughed. "No, you are not going to die, but you are about to learn a valuable lesson about eating things you know nothing about."

Granny would not let me wear underwear or pants because she didn't want to wash them, and she wanted the bran to run its course, so she told me to go bare-bottomed. I was shocked. I couldn't walk around naked from the waist down.

"There's nobody around to see you except family," she said matter-of-factly.

She gathered up all my clothes, and went to wash them in the river with soap. I was miserable. When she returned from the river I said, "Granny I can't walk around naked, I just can't."

"I don't care what you want. I am not washing your shitty clothes all day. You are wearing no underwear or pants until this is over."

She went into the house and left me standing there. I went into one of the barns, where I found some old towels she had piled there. I wrapped one around my waist like a skirt.

As I miserably walked around the farm, I would stop from time to time to pull the towel open and shit. I felt like one of the barn animals. I had to eat outside and sleep on the front porch at night because Granny said she was not washing any bedding or bed sheets.

For some reason, Granny's normally quiet farm life became very busy with people stopping by all the time. Every time I heard a car coming, my towel skirt and me would hide somewhere on the farm. I heard laughter from the visitors as Granny told them about her grandson getting into the pig bran and learning a valuable lesson.

To this day, I don't eat bran.

Allen and the Bees

It was late summer when Allen informed us he would be showing us the way to remove honey from an active beehive. I had no doubt the day would be eventful. Allen had been working as a farm hand for a local farmer, and he had watched the beekeepers pull out honeycombs all summer. For him, that was enough to assume he could do it himself. He wanted to share the first experience with us. Since he had been bringing honeycombs home with him almost every day from the farm, we all thought he knew what he was doing.

It was a beautiful sunny day when Allen informed us of his plan. We were all excited, as it was to be a new experience for us. We finished breakfast, and climbed into the truck. With all five of us in there, it was cramped, even with my little sister sitting on Marj's lap. There were no seat-belt laws back then, so we never bothered with them.

We always knew how long the trip was by the amount of beer Allen would bring with him. One to two bottles meant a short trip, and a case of beer meant a longer trip, with stopovers at people's homes. Today, he brought six beers so we knew the length was somewhere in between.

Allen had equipped himself with all the supplies he thought he needed: black garbage bags, leather gloves, rubber bands, a hat, pliers, a hammer, and few other things.

About an hour later we pulled up to the field. I could see white beehives in the corner of the field. Allen parked on the field, and started dressing himself to collect the honey. First, he put rubber bands around the cuffs of his pants and the sleeves of his shirt. Then, he buttoned his shirt up to his neck and put on his gloves. Finally, he grabbed two garbage bags and headed off to the hive, about fifty yards away.

He walked over to the middle hive and pulled one of the bags over his head so the bag covered him down to his waist. He proceeded to pull the lid cover off the top of the hive. Until the day I die I will never forget what happened next.

He pulled the cover off the hive, reached in and pulled out the honeycomb, dripping with honey and bees. As he started stuffing it into the second bag, bees poured out of the hive. The swarm came like a black cloud, completely encircling Allen. Instantly, he dropped the bag with the honeycomb and ran. The cloud grew larger as bees came out of every hive by the thousands. Allen did his best to escape those angry yellow and brown demons as he ran in a crazed zigzag. He couldn't see very well since the black bag was still over his head, and sometimes he ran back towards the hives. The buzzing of the bees was loud. It sounded like a gigantic, angry, unearthly flying machine.

We could see Allen waving his hands around his body and head in an attempt to keep the bees away. He finally managed to rip a hole at the top of the garbage bag so he could see where he was going. As he pulled his head through the hole, he spotted the truck and bee-lined (pardon the pun) towards us, with the swarm close behind. As Allen approached, the cloud of bees was so thick it blocked out the sun.

Marj started the truck and started driving away from Allen.

We could hear him screaming, "Wait! Wait! Don't leave me here, I want to get in!"

But Marj didn't stop. Terrified he'd get left behind, Allen got a spurt of adrenaline and managed to catch up with the truck and grab onto the large side-mirror. His face was pushed up to the window and bees crawled all over his head! He was screaming at Marj to stop the truck. His eyes bugged out of his face in pure terror and agony. The bees now started to come into the truck and flew around us. We started crying as they stung us.

Marj yelled at him to hang on because she was not stopping. She stepped on the gas as she tried to leave the bee cloud behind. Allen had no choice but to hang on and get dragged by the truck. He finally managed to pull his legs into the back of the pickup and lie there. Marj was speeding and weaving as fast as she could go. I looked through the back window at Allen wrapped up in his garbage bag with bees still hovering around him, his face swelling from the stings. This is the world's stupidest man, I thought, and he is my father. I see his swollen face to this day.

We never did get our fresh honey.

Kelly

When I was in grade four, we had been living in Whitelaw for a while. We weren't moving as much anymore so I was actually able to finish the whole grade in one school.

In late spring, Marj and Al brought home the most beautiful, adorable German Shepherd female pup. We named her Kelly. She had the cutest face and her ears stood straight up. As I look back, I remember her face as being regal, expressive of her great love and wisdom. Kelly was a huge hit with the family, since it was a good way to distract us from our unhealthy life.

Kelly became my best friend. We spent hours together and the hours turned into months as she grew up with us. At first she brought some peace to our family, because none of us could resist a puppy. Not even Al was immune to her charms.

It was one of the few times that I didn't dread leaving school at the end of the day - I actually ran home to play with her. She loved chasing frogs, so we spent hours hunting frogs and other creatures in the woods. We never killed the animals – I just held them for Kelly to sniff.

As she got older, she became very protective of my sisters and me. Allen had got it into his head that the best way to train her to be a watchdog was to beat her every day with a broom or whatever else was handy. When Kelly was about a year old, he started beating her every day. I screamed at him and asked why he had to beat my dog. He usually beat her in front of me, yelling, "This is how you train a dog."

How I hated my father for doing this. Yet I was unprepared for what he was about to do.

It was a summer day and the whole family was out in the yard. On a whim, Al decided that something I was doing was pissing him off, so he started beating me in front of Kelly, his back to her. At some point, Kelly leapt onto his back, attacking him. I remember the terrified look on his face.

Kelly got so mad she tore the shirt off his back, and he screamed for us to get her off. Finally, he managed to break free. He grabbed her by the collar and pulled her to the doghouse, chaining her. All the while, Kelly barked and growled, while we yelled at them both to stop.

Allen was completely enraged, almost frothing at the mouth. I had never seen him this angry and scared. I felt so good that something out there had stood up to Al when he was hurting us. I was so proud of Kelly and loved her with all my heart for protecting me.

"This won't fucking happen again!" He turned and headed into the house. Suddenly, my heart hurt, my stomach turned to mush, and fear coursed through my body. I even peed my pants. I knew what was coming.

I screamed at him. "No, *no*! It's okay, she didn't mean it, she won't do it again, I promise!"

Allen returned shortly with his double barrel shotgun, loading it as he walked. Now Marj started yelling at him not to do it. Al snapped the shotgun shut, and as we all screamed at him, he blew half of Kelly's head off in front of us. I can still smell gunpowder and hear the deafening noise.

Kelly's twitching body was in front of me, blood and brains coming out of the missing part of her proud, regal head. I was numb.

Alan yelled again, "You'll never fucking do that to me again."

I started crying and screaming at him. Marj stood there completely in terror - this was too much even for her to comprehend.

I ran, crying and throwing up, into the woods. While hiding there, I planned how I would take the same gun and blow his head off while he was asleep.

I felt deep inside that I had caused her death, that if I had not done anything to make Al mad, Kelly would still be alive. I didn't go back home that night.

The next morning I came home early to see Kelly's bloodied body still lying by the doghouse where she was shot. The pooled blood on the dirt was now thick and sticky and flies swarmed over the blood and around the missing part of her head. I threw up again.

THE SPOT WHERE KELLY WAS SHOT

Marj came outside and told me she needed my help to load Kelly into the back of the truck. We took her to the dump, where Marj backed up to the edge of the pile of garbage, opened the tailgate and threw my best friend into the dump.

I vowed then that I would never cry again or let anything or anyone close to me. I would never allow Allen to make me go through something like that again. No more pets. For years I wanted to kill Allen.

But I couldn't become like him. I could not, I would not. Something inside me told me I was different.

Picking Berries

I always enjoyed berry picking with Granny in the summer and fall. I had a habit of eating more than I picked. As the weeks went by, we picked whatever wild berries were ripe; each berry's season passed fairly quickly; strawberries, goose berries, choke cherries, raspberries and one of my favourites, Saskatoon berries.

We got up early to avoid the mid-day heat. Granny would gather all the plastic ice cream pails that she collected throughout the year, and tie them around my waist with an old pair of nylons.

In the springtime, we picked wild strawberries, and whatever we collected, Granny made into jams and preserves. Wild strawberries are tiny, most of them no bigger than your fingernail, but bursting with flavour. To this day, I have never tasted any farmed strawberries that have the intense flavour of wild strawberries. I stuffed myself before putting any berries into the pail! It took a lot of strawberries, and a long time, to fill an ice cream pail.

When the season came for Saskatoon berries, I got very excited. These berries were easier to pick and the bushes had no thorns on them. Granny made the best Saskatoon pie, so I was always diligent when picking. Plus, I got full faster and was ready to put the rest of the berries into the pail sooner than with the other berries.

One day, Granny and I were picking Saskatoons at one of our favourite bush areas. We would start on the same side and then pick berries going in opposite directions, making a circle around the bush.

We had just started picking, and I needed to fill myself first. The berries higher up on the bush were always ripest because they got more sun. I wanted to eat these first, so I reached up to collect them. I became completely absorbed, picking and eating, no longer aware of anything else going on around me.

I was moving to the left and picking berries high up to my right so I was not facing the direction in which I was moving. I heard a noise on my blind side, thinking it must be Granny. I continued, intent on my picking, when I bumped into something beside me that was big and felt furry.

"Granny is not wearing a fur coat." I thought.

I spun to the left to see what I had run into. Mere inches away, was the startled face of a black bear that was doing the same as I - eating Saskatoon berries. The bear made a startled woof. I think he was as surprised as I was!

I yelled for Granny, running to the right as the bear ran to the left. Granny came around the bush as I was screaming her name. I ran into her as I turned back, looking over my shoulder at the fleeing bear. She laughed out loud when she realized what had happened. She had seen the startled bear running across the field and me running from him, hollering. I shook like a leaf in the wind and clung to Granny for dear life. She pulled me off of her, still laughing. "That must have taught you a lesson. You have to pay attention out here. We're not the only ones picking berries!"

As I calmed down, I saw how funny the whole thing was. I had discovered that animals were just like us. They, too, got caught up in the moment. Granny assured me this didn't mean we were going home, so we finished our picking. Only this time, I never left Granny's side. She picked the higher berries and I picked the lower ones.

The next day, we went out to pick more. Before we left the house, she tied a big cowbell around my waist so she knew where I was, and the animals picking with us would know, too. I clanged at every motion. For the rest of the berry season, I sounded like a milk cow out to pasture.

Maw Puss

It was our first summer in Whitelaw. School was out and Marj decided to take all of us to Granny's farm for a few weeks. We were all very excited for the trip and were looking forward to seeing Granny, Granddad and the rest of the family. Allen stayed home, on his own, and told me he would take care of the animals. I had rabbits, chickens, ducks, and my cat. Maw Puss was a large, grey shorthair that was always pregnant. Marj used to say that Maw Puss would screw any tomcat in the country - a very ironic comment coming from her.

Maw Puss was the only pet I had left because of my father's rage. The rabbits and other animals were farm animals; they were not pets to me. Maw Puss loved me and I loved her. Every time I got a beating from Marj or Allen, she would come to me when I was in bed crying. She would lie by my head and purr, or rub her head against mine. Sometimes, she would lick my head when my face was buried in the pillow. Her tongue was very rough and felt like coarse sandpaper. I didn't care that it hurt a bit; she was doing all she could to comfort me.

I think I called her Maw Puss because she was like an animal mom to me. In my life, I always wanted to do well and be kind to everyone. My animals, even with their short life spans, greatly influenced me. My pets always showed others around them (including me) true love and kindness. I saw the abuse they received from my parents, and though they tried to stay out of Allan's way, they continued to live with us with love in their hearts. For a long time, I wondered why they didn't run away – they often could have. I realized if they could take all this abuse and still be able to love, then I could do the same.

Maw Puss liked to hunt at night. Sometimes she would bring mice and other animals to my bed for me to eat, just as she did for her kittens. I always took the offerings from her and waited until she had gone out again to dispose of them. I never wanted to insult her for her gifts - I think she thought I ate them.

Now, Maw Puss was pregnant again. I felt uneasy leaving her alone in that condition with Allen, and I told Marj, who told me to not worry. He had promised her that he would take good care of my animals, feeding and watering them every day. I wasn't worried about the outdoor animals. If he got drunk and forgot about them, they could take care of themselves for a few days. I knew he was never passed out for more than a couple of days at a time. When he got hungry, he got motivated to do things.

I was excited and uneasy at the same time when we finished packing up the truck and began the drive. It would take all day to drive to Granny's farm, since we lived in the northern part of the province and she lived in the very south. We waved to Allen and he waved back, smiling. I told myself to stop being so nervous, that everything would be okay.

Our trip was uneventful. Marj always seemed excited when we went to stay with Granny. It was a good break from Allen. Marj seemed happier, less moody, and she never hit us in front of Granny.

We had a great time at the farm, with lots of freedom and many happy memories.

I always felt sad to leave, as then I would be thrown back into reality. When we left for Granny's farm, we were quiet and became more excited, as we got closer. When we left the farm, we started off excited and happy, re-telling our favourite memory of our holiday. As we got closer to home we became quieter, and by the time we pulled into the driveway we were silent.

Allen was at the back door to greet us, and before we even went inside he said, "I've got some bad news for you about Maw Puss. She is dead."

My heart jumped into my throat, and my insides turned to water. I thought I was going to pee myself as fear seeped through me.

"Not Maw Puss!" I cried out. "What happened to her? Did she get hit by a car?"

"No," Allen said, "She went crazy after she had her kittens and tried to jump through your sister's bedroom window. She killed herself on the broken glass. I buried her in the back yard, I'll show you where."

"Oh," he added. "Her kittens are all dead but I can't find most of them. They must have crawled into the corners of the house and died."

My heart, my soul, my complete being, fractured at that moment. I realized beyond a doubt that he had killed her and the kittens. I ran past him towards my sister's bedroom. It was a mess and stank. I looked up at the window Maw Puss had tried to jump out. The upper window was broken to the width of the cat, and her grey fur and blood stuck to the shards of the jagged glass. Blood had dripped down along the lower window and the wall, collecting into a now-dried pool on the floor. I looked at the scene in total shock.

The bedding I had made for Maw Puss to have her kittens was covered with blood. It stank of urine and feces. I looked at my father as tears streamed down my face.

"Where did you bury her and the kittens?" I asked numbly.

"Follow me and I'll show you," he said.

I felt like I was in a trance. The family joined me and we followed him out past the chicken coops and sheds to a far corner of our large yard. He pointed down to the freshly turned up earth where a little wooden cross-marked the grave.

We all stared in disbelief. I could see the tears in Marj's eyes, and I felt like something had happened to her at that moment. This had shaken her down to her soul.

We finally went back to the house and unpacked in silence. Marj cleaned up the mess in the girl's bedroom and started making dinner.

I heard her say to Allen, "Why in the hell would a cat try to jump through a window? Unless you were doing something to make it want to jump out..."

He snapped back to her he didn't do a thing. He told her Maw Puss jumped out the window when he tried to change the sheets after she gave birth to the kittens.

"She started running around the room like crazy, jumping up on the dresser and then through the window. I left it just as it was so you could see it. I knew you would try to blame me for this."

"I'm not sure I believe you," she said.

"I don't care if you believe me or not. That's what happened," he retorted. I heard him slam the fridge door and open a beer before storming out of the house.

I lay on my bed in the living room and quietly cried. I could smell something in my pillow. I felt around and found three dead kittens hidden inside. Maw Puss must have brought them into my bed. Allen said the kittens had crawled away and died, but there was no way these kittens could have crawled onto my bed. They were barely a week old.

I lay in bed with the kittens in my hand, trying to imagine what had happened to Maw Puss and her litter. I imagined that during one of his drunken fits, Allen had hurt Maw Puss and her kittens. I imagined that Maw Puss had tried to save them by hiding them in my pillow.

I believe Allen threw her through the window while she was trying to save her babies. He must have thrown the other kittens around the bedroom wherever they were lying.

I held those kittens until I fell into a fitful sleep. The next day I got up early and took the dead kittens to Maw Puss's grave. I took a shovel and dug down in the earth until I could see Maw Puss's body outlined in the dirt. I did not want to dig her up. I just wouldn't be able to stand seeing her bloodied, broken body.

I picked up the kittens and laid them on top of her. Now her whole family was together again.

I stood there, crying, unable to believe what was lying in front of me. I covered Maw Puss and her family with earth.

Allen was a cruel and evil man. Would he kill one of us next?

Marj and the Dogs

It was early fall in Whitelaw. Marj had gone out to the sheds and had come running back, upset and scared. Three dogs in the sheds had barked and growled at her. At the time, we had some chickens, ducks and a few geese. I was not concerned for the animals since it was early morning and they were still locked up. I looked outside and saw a large, beautiful German Shepherd, a medium-sized mutt with patches of black, dark brown and white, and a small Terrier and Border collie mix. They ran around the cages, sniffing at the chickens, ducks and geese.

It seemed to me they meant no harm, but Marj was really distressed. She went out onto the porch, yelling at the dogs to go home. They just looked at her and started barking. It became a shouting match – she would yell and they would bark back.

After a while, the smaller dog went into our storage shed and the other dogs followed. Marj jumped off the landing and ran to the shed. She slammed the door shut and locked the bolt. I could hear the dogs barking inside and pushing against the door, trying to get out.

Marj came storming back into the house muttering, "These dogs will never do this again."

"Mom, what are you going to do?"

She looked at me as she headed to the bedroom where she and Allen kept their guns, and said, "What do you think?" She repeated herself, louder this time, "This is the last time they will do this to us."

That line sounded so horribly familiar. I recognized the sick wave that came over me.

She came out of the bedroom with the 22-calibre gun and began loading it full of shells, not one or two to scare the dogs off, but filling the gun completely. I knew Marj was a very good shot. She had taught me how to shoot at Granny's farm.

"Mom, please don't," I pleaded. I ran out after her into the yard.

I could see the shed door moving back and forth as the dogs tried to escape. Marj slid the safety off, put the rifle to her shoulder and aimed at the door. I was standing behind her on her left. I saw the dogs' noses poking out under the door. One nose stuck out ahead of the others, and Marj aimed just above it and shot. Immediately, the nose stopped moving. I think it was the German Shepard because it was the biggest nose of the three.

Marj quickly put another shell into the rifle's chamber and fired again at the next nose. That nose pulled back and I could hear yelping inside the shed. The third nose disappeared before Marj could put another shell in. I started to cry now.

She started shooting into the shed through the door, not knowing where the dogs were but firing again and again until the gun was empty. All we heard was whimpering, crying and faint yelps as the bullets found their targets. As tears streamed down my face, Marj reloaded again.

"Mom, please don't shoot them anymore, can't you hear them crying?" She didn't look at me as she reloaded.

"I told you they would never do this to us again," she repeated.

After she reloaded, Marj walked to the shed and opened it. As she did, the German Shepard's head rolled forward. She stood at the opened doorway with the rifle up against her shoulder, scanning the shed for movement. She heard a noise and quickly fired into the depths. There was no more movement after that. I had to will myself not to throw up, and swallowed the bile rising in my throat.

Marj completed a final survey of the shed, her rifle still ready to shoot at the slightest signal. Satisfied, she put down her rifle, and said, "We have to get these bodies out of here. These dogs belong to someone, and they'll come looking for them after they don't come home today. I'm going to back the truck up to the shed and we'll load the bodies into the back. You need to help me lift them."

SHED WHERE THE THREE DOGS WERE SHOT

She turned and headed back to the house, the rifle tucked under her arm. As I looked at the dogs, I thought I heard the little one whimpering quietly. As I bent over its body I heard its shallow breathing. I stroked its head and tears flooded my eyes. Once again, one of my parents had done terrible things to an animal.

I heard the truck door open and close. Marj pulled up to the shed and I studied her face. How could this person be my mother? She was a stranger to me.

She stopped the truck and came over to where I was standing. Together, we picked up the heavy German Shepherd. We had to swing him back and forth to get him into the back. As I helped, blood sprayed onto my hands and pants. We picked up the next dog and threw it in. As Marj pushed the two dogs further into the back, I went and picked up the smallest dog. Its breathing was even shallower now and it was going to die soon. I couldn't bring myself to tell Marj it was still alive because I knew she would just shoot it again, so I just quietly laid it down with the others.

The back of the truck was covered in blood, as was the ground in the shed. She slammed the tailgate shut and told me to get in. We drove in silence.

At the town dump, we pushed out the dogs. I pulled the little dog towards me. I picked him up and held him close to my chest. He was still alive, still breathing. I gently laid him by the other dogs. I felt very old and tired. We had now disposed of four dogs into the dump. I wondered to myself if one of us would end up at this same place the same way.

Marj threw me a rag and told me to clean myself up. She threw the rags on top of the dogs. Blood has a very heavy smell – it hung in the air around us. I've never forgotten that smell.

On Monday at school, some kids asked if anybody had seen their dogs. I mumbled no, then ran into the woods, crying.

Bikes and Freedom

While living in Whitelaw, I yearned to have my own bike. I asked, whined and begged Allen and Marj daily. All my friends at school had one, but it also meant I could explore on my own and escape the house, if need be.

I was so happy the day Marj and Allen brought home a used bike, although I was disappointed when I saw it. It was a girl's bike! I could live with the rust and the few dents and scratches but having a girl's bike was hard to take. I was told it was easier to learn on a girl's bike because there was no cross bar on it to 'rack' yourself on.

We were given a bit of instruction from Allen and Marj. I don't think they knew much about riding a bike. We were told how it worked and then sent on our own. We spent hours climbing on, then peddling a few feet and falling off. It was difficult on our gravel roads! When one fell off, the other would pick up the bike and the kid, and take their turn peddling until they, in turn, fell. It took days and lots of road rash before we finally mastered being on two wheels. My middle sister and I supported each other through this learning experience, often crying to the other with our road rash hurts. We felt close to each other during this time.

I got to ride my girl's bike to school with the other boys while Marj walked with the girls. The boys teased about the bike but I didn't care. This was my first taste of freedom. I could go where I wanted without having to depend on Marj or Allen.

I always let my middle sister ride it whenever she wanted to, so she wouldn't forget how to ride. I began saving for a real boy's bike. Eventually, I bought one from a school friend. His parents bought him a three-speed bike with a shifter on the cross bar and a big tall 'sissy' bar on the back. I paid twenty dollars for my new bike, and I was so proud when I rode home on it. I gave the girl's bike to my sister. Now, we both had bikes and freedom.

Locked Out

On a bitterly cold winter afternoon we arrived home from school to find the front and back doors locked and no one home. Allen was away working for a few months, so Marj could come and go as she pleased.

We had no key. We tried all the ground floor windows but they were nailed shut for the winter months, so no cold air would get in.

My sisters started to cry, as it got darker and colder. We had been playing in the snow after school. Our gloves and clothes were wet and frozen, and we were shivering. I took the girls to a shed in the yard. It wasn't heated and the boards were wooden and sparse, but it had a roof, and we could huddle together in the hay. We sat together in one of the corners and pulled grain sacks over us, trying to get warm.

I gave my toque and gloves to my sisters, rubbing my now bare hands together to try and warm them up, without success. My sisters cried quietly and asked how long it would be until Mom came home to let us in. I didn't know any more than they did but I told them it would be soon and they shouldn't worry. Sometimes, if she was with one of her boyfriends, she didn't return until early morning.

Because we lived in a cold climate, we had been taught the basics of survival at school - staying together, keeping as warm as possible and never falling asleep. I didn't want to upset my sisters so I didn't mention not falling asleep, but I told stories and jokes, desperately wanting to keep us awake.

Around midnight we heard a car drive up to the house - its headlights shone through the holes in the shed walls. We all jumped up and ran out. The girls cried and hung onto her arms as she unlocked the door.

We had been outside for six hours and we got no apology. She simply told us to put on our pajamas and get ready for bed. We ate cold cereal for dinner, and that was the end of it.

I lay there, fuming. What the hell was wrong with my Mom? The next day, after Marj went out, I pulled the nails out of the bathroom window and practiced opening and closing it, so I was sure it was possible to get in. If there were a next time, we wouldn't be locked out again.

Leaving Whitelaw

Shortly after Allen had killed Maw Puss, her kittens and Kelly, Granny and others urged Marj to leave. One day, after she had visited Granny, she came back talking about a secretive plan. She didn't know when she would do it, but the day would come. We wouldn't be able to take much – just the necessities. We had to pack our clothes, boots, and gloves first, and if there was room, we could take toys and other things. I made sure to pack my comics and books with my clothes - they had been my world for so long and I couldn't leave them behind.

Marj told us to keep our stuff neat from now on so that if the chance came to leave, we would be ready immediately. We had to be careful not to do or say anything to make Allen suspicious. He was working for a farmer in the area and worked longer days during the summer. The plan was for us to finish the school year and leave that summer. We lived on pins and needles not knowing when Marj would tell us to pack up.

As the summer days grew longer, Marj got more agitated and nervous. I knew the day for us to leave was coming soon. She had found out from Allen that he would be working sixteen-hour days getting the hay feed off. After he'd eat and have a few drinks, he wouldn't want to drive back and forth from home. When Allen left for work the next morning, Marj seemed calmer. When he left, we knew he would not be home for two to three days. I knew this would be the day we would leave.

Shortly after Allen left the house, she told us to pack up. We were going to drive to Red Deer, the next city over. After we had stripped the house bare, we walked through the house together.

"We're never coming back, are we?"

Marj looked down at me, tears in her eyes, and said softly, "No, Greg, we are never coming back."

As we left the house I discovered an old skeleton key that locked the door between the living room and kitchen – I liked to lock it when my sisters and I were alone in the house. When everyone was out of the house, I closed the door and locked it, taking the key with me. I don't know why I did it. Allen returned home three days later to discover he was locked out. Later, family members told me he became so enraged by our leaving that he kicked and ripped the locked door off its hinges.

After we loaded everything into the pick-up truck, the one that had taken Kelly to the dump, Marj covered the boxes in back with a tarp. We climbed in and drove away. I looked back at the old house that had forever changed our lives and thought of Maw Puss and Kelly dying because of me. I felt sad thinking I would never come back to the yard where Maw Puss was buried. I started to cry.

After driving for about half an hour, Marj became nervous, telling us to look for grain trucks, as Allen drove the farmer's truck on the same road. This was the only road out of Whitelaw to the highway and it was the most risky place for us to be caught. After we turned on to the highway, Marj's shoulders and body relaxed and she slumped down. We both knew the terrible beatings we would receive if we got caught or worse.

Marj became happier, and we starting singing along with the radio to 'Uncle Albert / Admiral Helmsly' by Paul McCartney's band, Wings. Whenever the song came on, Marj would crank up the sound and sing along again.

I asked Marj where we were going, where would we be staying, were we safe from Dad? Marj explained everything she did to prepare. Granny had helped her contact social services and the department of welfare. We would stay in a welfare house once we got to Red Deer. I remember visiting the city once - it was quite big. It made me feel scared. Marj said that she contacted a lawyer to file for divorce, and she notified the Red Deer RCMP about what he had done to our pets and us.

The police told Marj and Granny they would locate Allen and tell him if he contacted us or came near us, they would arrest him. Marj assured me he would not hurt us ever again. I had helped Marj carefully load all the guns and ammo we owned into the truck before we left. I knew she meant it. She said that different people from the government would be talking to us about Allen, and all I had to do was tell them the truth.

She told me, "As far as I'm concerned, he will never be part of our lives in any way."

I thought of how I would now have to adjust to a new school with new teachers, new kids, and new friends. And who were these government people that were going to be asking questions? I had to start all over again. Would it ever stop?

Red Deer

Moving to Red Deer

We drove all day that day in early July 1973, and were met by Granny at our new house. We were nervous and excited about our new life, hopeful that our damaged family would have a new beginning.

OUR HOUSE IN RED DEER, ALBERTA

Our new house was old and a bit run down but we didn't complain. All that mattered was we were away from Allen and the house was ours.

We didn't have much money, so I got a paper route a month after we moved. Our family needed every penny, so it helped pay half our food bills.

That fall, I began grade five at Central Elementary School. I still loved school. I worked hard, and before long, my teachers were happy to see me excel. In that sense, I fit right in.

When it came to being sociable, I fell into my old, aloof patterns. I hadn't really learned how to be friends with kids during my previous school years, and I was afraid people would find out about my volatile family history. The less they knew about us, the better.

Our house was a block away from the public swimming pool. My sisters and I spent most of our summer there. As a family, we started to become calmer, with Allen out of our lives.

The quiet calm came to a screeching halt when the day we dreaded came. It was September and we were home making dinner when we heard a knock on the door. Marj answered it. It was warm out, so our front door was open, with the screen door keeping bugs out.

We heard her swear aloud before slamming the front door shut. She yelled for us to lock the back door and stay away from the windows. She ran back into the kitchen, grabbed the phone and called the RCMP.

Allen banged on the door and windows. He was yelling that he was not mad at us. He just wanted to talk to her and to the kids - we could work it out.

My sisters hugged each other. It felt like the monster from our nightmares was real and outside our house, trying to get in. His arrival scared my youngest sister so much she went and got the shotgun out of Marj's closet. She pointed it at him through the window he was banging on. The gun was not loaded but Allen didn't know that, so he quickly backed away.

At that moment, two police cars stopped in front of our house. Policemen got out and ran over to Allen. They led him away from the house, back to the sidewalk near their cars. Allen was distressed and began arguing with them. The police told Allen he was not allowed anywhere near us. If he came back or bothered any of us at school or anywhere else, they would arrest him.

Marj was standing behind the front door, watching through a small slot. One of the officers left the men and walked over to the house. Marj opened the door to talk to him. He told her everything was okay and that Allen was informed of the restraining order.

I watched Allen continue to argue. Suddenly, the cop pulled out his handcuffs and threatened to arrest Allen on the spot. When he saw the cuffs, Allen looked scared and stopped arguing. From his reaction, I realized he had been arrested before. He was escorted to his parked truck across the street and the police watched him drive away.

The cops remained parked in front of our house for about fifteen or twenty minutes to make sure he didn't circle back and return to the house. Before leaving, they told Marj to lock the windows and doors. If Allen came back, she should call them right away and they would arrest him.

I had seen police come to our house countless times in my early life to stop a violent fight. They never did anything other than tell my parents to knock it off. For the first time, I was glad to be visited by police.

Allen must have realized these RCMP officers meant what they said – they would follow through and arrest him if he didn't listen. They were different from the small town police Allen usually dealt with.

We didn't see Allen for the rest of the summer, but I'm sure he stalked and shadowed us.

We gradually fell into a comfortable routine. As summer wound down, we looked forward to going back to school again. We all hoped and prayed that this would be the end to all the pain and toxicity. We even started meeting other kids in the neighbourhood and hanging out.

September came quickly. Grade five was exciting because the school had different classes based on the student's skill level. What that really meant was there were classes for the smart, average or dumb. Within a few months, I was in every accelerated class in my grade, and I continued grade six the same way.

As grade six approached, my parents' divorce was coming to a close. My sisters and I had to meet the judge handling our parents' divorce. He wanted to know our stories of the abuse and what had happened within our family. My heart sank when Marj told me Allen was seeking custody of us. I wondered why he wanted us.

I remember in great detail the day we had to see the judge. We were asked to speak separately. I was led into his chamber and he rose from his desk and shook my hand. He was a little short, had glasses and a kind face and eyes. He was wearing his judge's robe and looked very important. I knew this was serious and I had to tell this man the truth. He tried to make me feel at ease and asked about school and what sports I played. He asked me if I had friends at school. I was happy to tell him I had found friends for the first time in my life.

He then asked what had gone on in our family. He was holding a package of papers that he continually looked at while we spoke. He read me some of the stories of abusive episodes and asked me if they were true. After each question, I honestly confirmed they were. After each of my responses he took notes.

Finally, he told me he was going to ask an important question that would affect my future. He told me to think about it before answering right away and I nodded. He told me Allen really wanted to raise me - he would let the girls live with Marj, and I would live with him. Allen had told the court that a boy belonged with his father, and promised I could see Marj and my sisters anytime I wanted. That meant I would not live in Red Deer - I would go back to Whitelaw with him, and we might move down to the Innisfail area in a few years.

I broke out in a cold sweat and started to shake and cry. I knew in my heart and soul that if I lived with Allen, I would be dead in less than a year. I knew that Allen would try to get back at Marj, and he wanted me as his tool for revenge. I told the judge that if I went with Allen, I knew I would be seriously hurt or even killed. He looked startled by my reaction and comment.

He read more of the documents. "These are serious things you are saying about your father." I just nodded at him.

He looked at me in silence and then said to me in a kind, soft voice, "You and your family have been through a lot. I will rule that you stay together as a family. I'm going to deny Allen's request for custody. Do you want him to visit?"

I said no. The judge thanked me for my honesty, and asked me to send in my middle sister.

The judge talked to each of my sisters and in the end, ruled for us to stay together as a family, minus Allen. Everything was fantastic for me until one morning in early October 1974, when I could not get out of bed.

Spinal Damage

My spinal damage occurred when we were still living in Whitelaw. I was lying on the floor in the living room, petting my cat and watching television. I heard Allen's truck pull into the driveway. I could always tell he was drunk by the way he pulled in and parked. I heard his unsteady footsteps on the gravel as he approached the door. Marj was in the kitchen and I heard her bitching at him for coming home drunk again. I heard the fridge door open, and heard Allen taking the cap off a beer. As he walked into the living room, he saw me lying there. I looked up at him as his eyes narrowed. He drew back his leg and said, "Get the fuck out of the way!"

He brought his leg down and kicked me in the lower back. I flew through the air and landed in the corner of the living room. Unbearable pain went through my body and I began to cry.

Marj came running from the kitchen. "What hell is going on?" That always seemed like a common phrase in our family. She crouched over me, asking him why he had kicked me.

Allen shrugged his shoulders and sipped his beer. "He was in the way. Can't he sit on the fucking couch?"

His kick had been strong enough to shift the spine in my lower back. I didn't realize that the damage was even more serious than the usual beatings. I was in pain all the time, almost every day, so it was hard to trace the pain back to something specific. After the kick, my spine began to grow crookedly; until the pressure on my lower spine was so great I couldn't walk anymore. It took a year for this spinal damage to appear from when I was kicked across the room by Allen in Whitelaw. Now, living in Red Deer, I woke up one morning, and I could not physically get out of bed.

Marj, at first, thought I was joking, but when she saw my pain she took me to Red Deer General Hospital Emergency for x-rays. The x-rays showed severe spinal damage located in the lower area of my back, right where Allen had kicked me. Because of the spinal damage, the doctors worried I would never be able to walk again.

The doctors had a new treatment for spinal traction, so instead of drilling pins into my hips, they used a girdle and cable system attached to weights to pull my spine true. I was in traction for eight weeks, unable to leave my bed.

Sometimes, the other kids in the pediatric ward would come by and take some weights off on one side and add them to the other one. This would pull me sideways in the hospital bed, and I would have to yell to the nurses to come in and even out the weights.

For two months, I was completely bed-ridden. The nurses were caring and loving. I had never been treated that way before by anyone other than Granny. I was fed three times a day with better food than what I got at home. There were games and toys I had never seen before to play with.

Teachers from my school came by every Friday to drop off schoolwork. Since I couldn't get up or enjoy recess and have a normal school schedule, I would complete all my schoolwork in about two days. The nurses brought their kids' homework for me to do as well, since they saw how bored I was. I often thought how great it would be if I could stay in the hospital after I was better.

One day, a nurse told me it was time for x-rays to see if the traction device had worked. My spine was much better.

"It's time to learn how to walk again," she told me. I thought she had lost her mind. Walking was the easiest thing in the world – I had done it all my life.

As she prepared the wheelchair, I threw back the covers and rolled myself to the edge of the bed. Instead of my legs swinging over and touching the floor as I had expected, they didn't move. I fell flat on my face onto the hard concrete floor. I lay there, moaning that I couldn't move my legs, and wanting to die. I hated my life and all that happened to me, and now I couldn't walk.

The nurse yelled for staff to come help me into my wheel chair.

"Don't worry," she reassured me. "It's normal to lose the use of your legs after being in traction for such a long time. You are going to do a lot of work to get them moving again."

We went to the rehabilitation room. There were two parallel bars, like the ones in gymnastics, but closer to the ground. The nurse rolled my wheelchair to the end of the bars. I had to pull myself up and 'walk' between the bars, dragging my legs behind me like two useless limbs. I hated it, and just hung there between the bars wishing myself to die, but my nurse would not take 'no' for an answer. I felt like a cripple. She pushed, begged, joked, hugged and cried for me to walk again. I wish I could remember her name.

It took almost a month for me to recover the full use of my legs, and strengthen my spine. We went to the rehab room day in and day out, and on days she wasn't there, she had another nurse work with me. She also was determined that I would walk again.

Before discharging me, the doctors put a body cast on me to keep my spine straight and prevent any further injury. The cast started below my neck and stopped above my hips. It was like wearing body armour from the days of King Arthur. I had to wear this body cast for eight weeks to allow my spine to heal in a straight line. The doctors were very happy with my progress. I was their miracle boy.

The entire incident continued for a year, including the therapy I had to go through after the body cast was removed.

There were a few times I liked my body cast. Once, there was a tough guy in our school named Trevor. I told Trevor one day that I had been working on my stomach muscles and they were hard as a rock. I told him he could hit me as hard as he could in the stomach.

He said, "Bullshit, you're going to cry and get me in trouble."

I assured him I wouldn't, so he pulled back his right fist and hit me as hard as he could. The force of the punch knocked me off my feet and onto my back, but the yelling and screaming was coming from Trevor. It was a sweet moment for me.

The second best thing for my body cast was doing the 'dog pile', where everyone piled onto each other. It was a big thing at school with the guys. No matter how many kids piled onto me, my armour always protected me.

It was a sad day when the doctors took away my armour. I felt naked without it. I was back to being a normal, vulnerable and scared boy.

God and the Church

One summer when I was in grade six or seven, I asked Granny about God and the church, as I was confused about her opinions.

Granny loved her tea and stories in the afternoons. That day, she told me to wait until the stories were over and she would answer my questions as best as she could. I agreed and went outside to the barn, leaving her alone, and trying to organize the questions in my mind.

I eventually made my way to the house, where I heard her putting the teapot away. She came out soon with her cap on her head.

"Follow me. I've got some things to do on the pig barn. You can ask me your questions while I'm fixing the stalls."

When we got to the stalls, Granny collected the tools she needed. She was very self-reliant. If she needed anything done for her animals she did it on her own.

It was mid-spring and her piglets were about a month old. They were like naughty children, always pushing and chewing at the boards in the stalls, trying to get out. It was a constant struggle between Granny and those piglets – both sides were stubborn and knew how to get what they wanted.

The piglets made me laugh. Not only were they playful and curious, but also they seemed to encourage each other to cause mischief. They were a team of rascals; they had much more adventure than one pig could ever have on his own.

Granny found the last of the nails she needed, and then headed to the damaged pig stall. She turned to me. "What is it you need to know?"

"Well Granny," I said, choosing my words carefully. I still hadn't thought of a nice way to ask my question. "You said that people who believed in God go to church all the time and you hardly ever go to church. You only go on special occasions or if there's a wedding, or when someone dies."

She nodded and pointed for me to pass her the saw. She wanted to cut off the bottom of the chewed up board.

"That's right, I've said that."

She marked the length of the new board with a nail and picked up the handsaw.

"So what is it you need to know?"

"So, do you always believe in God or just when you go to church?" I nervously asked. I saw in her eyes that she understood my question. She turned and finished nailing the new board to the bottom of the pig stall. The piglets' escape was postponed, at least for one more day.

"There you go, you buggers - chew on that one for awhile."

She gathered up her tools and headed out of the stall. I followed her.

"You didn't fully understand what I was saying. People that believe in God go to church to show other people who believe in God that there are others like them out there. When we moved to our farm, all the farmers were so isolated that we wouldn't see anyone for weeks or months on end. On special occasions, the neighbours would get together at church. It was a time for sharing – there was food, laughter. Everyone caught up with each other's lives. We were there to support each other. It was a tough life. As a community we felt better, knowing that we were all farmers, and church was the place to bring everyone together."

She turned and put the tools back into her toolkit. "I want to show you something."

We walked around the barnyard and she pointed to the Red Deer River flowing by.

"Every time I see the river, I see God. See the hills on both sides of us?" she said, pointing. I nodded.

"When I see the hills, I see God. When I see clouds, thunder and lighting, when I see the sun and the moon, I see God. God is all around us, all the time when I see those little buggers chewing and ripping my stalls apart, I see God. You do not have to go to church every Sunday to believe in Him. Some people go to church every Sunday pretending to believe in God. You carry God with you in your heart and everything you see and hear around you is God's way to remind you of his presence. Do you understand what I'm saying to you?" she asked. She looked at me to make sure I did.

"Yes, Granny I understand what you are saying," I said nodding my head.

"Church is for all of us to come together, show support, and to hear God's word spoken by the Minister, who works for God. Remember, a lot of farmers can't read or write and need to hear the words of God from someone who can. I also have my own Bible and I read from it every day. This way I can see, hear and be surrounded by God's presence, and I can read God's word anytime I want to. Greg, this is believing in God. I think it's time you read the Bible. I'll make you a deal. Read the Bible like one of your books. Don't read it thinking it's a Bible, read it like one of your mystery or detective books you've been reading. When you're finished, we'll talk about it."

It was the start of a long, hot summer on the farm. I had also read just about every book there. "OK, Granny, I'll read it."

"Good," she said. "Now help me gather the eggs and we'll start getting things ready for supper."

I was very happy with Granny's answer. Granny always spoke the truth. Sometimes the truth she spoke came out harshly, only because it was a harsh truth coming from a tough situation.

Over the next month I worked at reading the Bible. It was extremely difficult and boring to begin with. I constantly asked Granny how to pronounce a name or word, or sometimes I'd ask her the meaning of some of the passages. It was hard work. After getting into the rhythm a bit and getting used to the King James's language, what with all the thy's, thees, forthwith's, theist's and all, it was a pretty good book; lots of murder, mayhem, bad guys and good guys, wars and battles, angels and demons, plagues. It was an exciting book, believe it or not.

When I had finished, Granny and I had many discussions about the stories. I asked her why some parts of the book seemed to be missing. When the Bible is read as a story, there are gaps and missing pieces as if some pages were simply removed. She told me the Bible was written by men, for men, so they could have control over everything. There was information they didn't want people to know, especially women. She believed that some of the missing information would have helped women.

While Granny did support the church, she had some objections about how the church treated women. Women who joined and worked for the church were treated in a way she didn't like.

Granny was not only very spiritual but also practical. She told me there were things in the world you could change and some things you simply could not.

Sweetums

When we first moved to the safe house in Red Deer, the house had a leaky roof, so Marj contacted the owner, who sent a carpenter to repair it. This carpenter, Sweetums, became part of our lives from that day forward. He and Marj dated for about a year, after which we moved into his house in Oriole Park, a subdivision in Red Deer. He seemed a decent man. Even though he was 6'2" and over 200 pounds, he did not hit people. He tried to be a father figure to my sisters and me, and a good partner for Marj.

When I turned fourteen, he helped me get my first hunting license. He took me duck hunting every fall. He also taught me how to raise tropical fish. Even now, I still have tropical fish. He also helped me to strengthen my body. I played no sports while living with Allen and Marj. I always read or played quiet games. Sweetums bought me weights, springs and a punching bag and helped me with weight training. This made me feel better and I enjoyed my newfound strength.

Granddad and Granny liked him, and thought he was good for Marj. He was calm, had a sense of humour, and made good money. He always had new cars and toys. I remember a motor home, sporting equipment, new guns, nice furniture, color TV and stereo system.

He taught me about the better things in life.

One day, he met and got the best of Allen. I was in Grade 8, and he and Marj went to a rodeo in Innisfail, twenty minutes south of Red Deer. In the crowd, they spotted Allen. He and Marj waited until the rodeo was over and everyone was leaving. Then they snuck up behind Allen. Sweetums lined himself up directly behind him. Without warning, he drove his fist into the back of Allen's head. The force of the blow knocked Allen off his feet and he landed face first onto the hard ground.

Marj told us Allen jumped up and started to ask why he was hit, but stopped when he saw Marj. Allen gathered himself up and hurried away, with Sweetums and Marj calling him names. Sweetums yelled at Allen that if he wanted a real fight, not beating up women and kids, that he would be happy to oblige.

However, after awhile, Sweetums and Marj's relationship started to fall apart. He became demanding and made accusations and Marj and he would fight. I think Marj liked drama and trauma. She must have had mental or chemical imbalance issues because of her wide mood swings. Sometimes when we came home, we didn't know whether we should be ducking or hugging when meeting Marj.

After a major argument, they broke up and we moved from his house to West Park, another Red Deer subdivision. Marj had been working as a secretary and had some money saved up. She bought a new low-income priced unit in a six-plex. Once again, I was starting a new school. I was in Grade 8, going to West Park Junior High School.

THE SCHOOL I ATTENDED IN RED DEER, ALBERTA

Marj and Sweetums stayed apart for about a year, reuniting again when I entered Grade 9. This time Sweetums moved in with us, renting out the house we used to live in.

During grade nine, I was still attending West Park Junior High School.

I first became aware of the anger in my head one day in a math class. There was this neighbour kid we hung around with. One day we were friends, the next he was on my case, being an asshole. This went on for a year and a bit. One day in class, our teacher, who was the principal, was called away to the office on business. When this happened, he left the class alone and sometimes didn't return. This particular day, my 'friend' was sitting at the desk in front of me. He started bothering me, shoving things off my desk and pushing the desk around with me in it. He was bigger than me, as usual. Finally, he grabbed me and pulled me, then slapped my face. I became enraged, jumped up out of my desk and grabbed him by the shirtfront. I pushed him up the aisle towards the front of the class. I was so angry that everything around my vision was red and blurry. All I felt was, "I have had enough of this shit."

My rage made me so powerful that I drove this student through the wall into the next classroom. We landed in a pile beside the stunned teacher and classroom full of students. I was so pumped up on adrenaline that I began shaking uncontrollably, and felt sick to my stomach.

Just when the dust was settling from the hole in the wall, the principal came back to the classroom. He stared at us in disbelief.

"What the fuck is going on here? Greg, Art, what the fuck were you two doing to cause this damage? The both of you to my office. Now!"

Art and I were as stunned as everyone else. I did not expect to drive him through the wall. We walked in silence to the principal's office and sat outside waiting to be punished. I kept thinking, "Where did this violence come from?"

The impending punishment scared me, but what I had done moments before scared me more.

When the principal arrived, we followed him into his office. We managed between us to make up a story that it was an accident - that we were goofing off around the desk area, and had been play-wrestling and fallen into the wall. We said we were sorry. The principal bought our story and told us that we had to share the expenses for repairing the wall. We agreed and left his office, relieved.

As I walked slowly home, I replayed in my head what had happened. This was my real first awareness of the anger and rage inside me. I was proud of myself! No one had ever stood up for me! Not even me! I wasn't sure how to handle this, so I ignored it. If I were to talk to someone, where would I start? What could they do for me?

I later became aware how jealous and envious I was of boys that had dads, even more so when the dads were good guys. These men loved their wives and kids. The kids would always brag about their fathers, which is what I imagined you were supposed to do. I always felt like an outsider.

I finished Grade 9, and looked forward to going to high school. I wasn't nervous, since I was used to starting at new schools. In Grade 10, I was quiet, kept my nose to the books, and did well in school. I was puzzled and confused by the teachers in high school. Many teachers did not care if you passed or failed, as there were too many students - well over 2,000 - to deal with.

In Grade 10, sometimes the tough kids would turn me upside down, put me head first into a garbage can, and roll it down the hallway. I was constantly pushed and shoved in the hallway, or locked into lockers, where I would have to wait to be let out by someone from the office. I never named names, as it would have made it worse to report them.

I was a perfect victim for teasing and bullying. I was distant from my family, had no friends, and was always seen alone. I never joined any games during or after school. I was always in the library and did well at school. Many kids wouldn't play with me or even acknowledge me because of my parents. I didn't want to endanger my only safe place, school, so I just went deeper into my head. I learned to take my classmates' abuse. Compared to my parents, the pain inflicted by my classmates never came close.

Some of these bullies were big men. Some were over six feet tall, well over 200 pounds and strong. They were hockey and football players, and farm boys. Even some of the teachers were scared of these men.

These bullies had no idea what I had gone through in my life. I wonder if they would have been surprised to find out I owned sixteen guns, rifles and shotguns.

Sometimes, I would fantasize about going home, loading up my guns and shooting every fucking bully that had made my life miserable. They had no idea that I could load my rifles, and with my scopes, I could shoot and kill these assholes from 300 yards away. I was an expert shot and they would never know who had done it.

It was teachings from my Granny, my girlfriend and her loving family, and my own internal fortitude that stopped me from carrying out these fantasies.

Granddad Washes the Dishes

That summer on Granny's farm, Granddad and I were left on our own while Granny was away for a week.

Granddad was not the world's greatest cook. Breakfast was toast and porridge, lunch was sandwiches and dinner was stew or whatever we managed to pull together.

Granny always cleaned up the kitchen and dishes after every meal, but Granddad only got around to it at night, just before he went to bed. He always stayed up later than I did, as he enjoyed watching Johnny Carson.

He usually got up between ten and noon. When I woke every day, I'd find the kitchen clean and the dishes washed and in their place. I mentioned to Granddad that we could clean up like Granny did after each meal instead of waiting until night. He laughed and said that it wasn't a problem to do it at night.

I felt guilty after four days of not helping with dishes, so on the fifth day I said I would clean up.

He laughed. "Well, if that is what you want to do, go ahead."

He paused. "Here, watch me and I'll show you how I wash and dry."

We had just finished dinner, and the sink was full. Still laughing, he put all the dishes, pots and pans on the floor. Then he opened the front door and whistled. Almost instantly, his two dogs, Sport and Lucky, came running. They went straight to the dishes and licked them clean. Granddad looked at me, still chuckling. "This is how I've been cleaning up for the last week! My stomach churned. I felt nauseous knowing that I had been using dishes, forks, spoons and knives that had all been cleaned by the incessantly eager tongues of Sport and Lucky. I didn't know what to say.

From them on, I washed my own dishes, and kept them separate from the rest of what Granddad had 'washed and dried'.

When Granny got back from her holiday, I told her what had been going on with our dishwashers. She pulled out all the dishes in the cupboards and put them into a sink filled with hot, soapy water.

"Oh, the old fool always does that when I'm away. I forgot to tell you about the way he cleans up. Whenever I come home, I always wash all the dishes myself."

She paused. "Lucky and Sport are always sad when I come home because they know their treat days are over!"

Moving Out

When we first moved to West Park, Marj told us she had qualified for a loan, and she was buying the end unit of a sixplex. It was a two-story house. The bedrooms were downstairs, and the bottom floor was for the kitchen, living room and laundry room. It was brand new. We had never lived in a new house before – it was so exciting for us.

The street we lived on was called, of all things, Whiteside Crescent.

Why was Alberta so fond of this word 'white'?

Our new school was West Park Junior High. It was across the football field from the house, and we could walk there in less than five minutes. There were four complexes in our neighbourhood, with six units per complex. Low-income single mothers purchased many of the units.

The complex was full of kids of all ages, from infants to teenagers. I made many friends, most of whom I would see all the way through high school. It was one of the first times in my school life that was stable. I went from middle school to high school with the same classmates.

When we moved, we thought Marj's mood swings would even out. But Marj always needed drama, trauma and commotion in her life. She fought with other single moms in the neighbourhood over stupid things such as parking, noise - anything to stir up hostility.

She never worried about where I was most of the time and I never spent much time at home, only showing up for a place to eat or to sleep. Usually I was at friends' homes.

I was quickly becoming independent, and finally, I had real friends. I was gone from sunrise to sunset, visiting them.

Money was always tight and I continued with my paper route, but when I turned thirteen I wanted to do something different. One day, I rode my bike to Revelstoke Building Supplies, nearby where we lived. I asked one of the clerks if they had any work or cleaning to be done.

He said he didn't need anything but would ask other staff if they might. He left and came back with Ron, who told me he needed a few garden sheds put together for display in front of the store. They were metal storage sheds, and they were set up in the backyard. The sheds were 'flat-packed', which I found out meant they were in a flat cardboard box, unassembled.

He had six awaiting assembly and would pay me fifty dollars a shed if I could build them without any damage. They were to be displayed, so they had to look perfect. He said they would provide all tools, and pay me upon each shed's completion.

"Just ask one of the yardmen to pull out a shed for you and give you whatever you need to get started."

I came in everyday after school, taking almost three and a half days to build the first shed. The next shed took me two and a half days to build - the third shed took one day. I now had a system and could build two sheds at the same time. That Saturday, I went to the lumberyard and built two sheds in one day. On Sunday, I told Ron he owed me one hundred dollars.

"Fucking hell, you built two sheds in one day? I don't believe it, show me."

He followed me to the back, saw the sheds and whistled. "I don't believe it. We could use some help around the yard, restacking lumber piles, cleaning up garbage and sweeping up. You still need to build us one more shed as part of our deal, but when you're done we'll hire you as a yardman. You can work here every day after school until closing and on Saturdays. We can use the extra help on Saturdays because all the homeowners come in for building supplies."

He laughed and said, "We can't keep paying you fifty dollars a shed at two a day. You'd be making more money than any of us when you work it out!"

The next day I started work as a yardman at $1.15 per hour. I got $10.00 tip per shed I built after I was a regular employee. No one at the store could build a shed as fast as I. Revelstoke could sell a shed on Saturday morning, charge the assembly fee and promise it built and delivered the same afternoon. They would put me on it and within three to four hours after the sale, the shed was built and delivered. Sometimes, I was sent to the house and would build it in the backyard.

The staff at Revelstoke liked me, and I enjoyed working there. I learned a lot about construction because of the building materials they sold. I became familiar with their language and terminology. Working in a lumberyard was a real education. People I worked with were called yard staff. There was office or desk staff, as well. These people wrote up the building package orders. The form would go the Yard Forman, who would then assign it to some of the yard staff for shipping.

The summer after that, I stopped going to Granny's for the summer. I was entering grade nine and began working full-time as a swamper. A swamper leaves the lumberyard with the truck driver and helps unload deliveries. I unloaded building packages, windows, doors, fireplaces and so on. I liked the freedom of going to different places and seeing new things. I met many different co-workers because the yard staff had a high turnover. After two years, I was the longest serving employee in the yard.

I remember Dan, a truck driver from the US, who had served in the Navy. He was fun but a bit crazy with his drinking, partying, smoking dope, and chasing women. One day, we were in the back of the lumberyard where no one could see us, and everyone was drinking beer, our usual after-work habit.

Have you ever smoked dope?" asked Dan.

I was fifteen at the time and had not. He pulled out a metal pipe and a chunk of black hash with white veins running through it. He broke a piece off the chunk, put it into the pipe and lit it. He took a few puffs and passed it around. Everyone took a puff or two until the pipe came to me. At first, I wasn't sure what to do. I remembered stories about the evil of drugs.

"Come on, take a hit," everyone said.

I took a couple of puffs and began coughing and hacking. After a few minutes I started to feel weightless, and a floating feeling came over my entire body. I began to sweat and felt nauseous. The conversation of the group swirled around me. One voice felt very close and another seemed miles away. I felt scared so I got up and walked to my bike, parked at the fence.

I felt like throwing up and wanted to get out of there as soon as possible. I could not pedal my bike so I walked it home along the creek behind the store. I felt dizzy and threw up just after getting to the creek, then threw up every 20 or 30 feet. I became so scared I thought I would have to turn myself in to the hospital.

It seemed like every footstep was in slow motion. After an hour of struggling along the creek, I felt better. I went home and tried to eat something but couldn't. I just went to my room and slept until the next morning. I did not like Dan after that. I found out later that the white veins in the hash were opium!! For the next few years, I would not smoke pot or hash. I wanted no part of it.

Over the next two years, I learned to operate the forklifts and drive the trucks around the yard. If the yard was lacking staff, the yard foreman would send me, at fifteen with my learner's license, to drive and deliver smaller loads in the one-ton truck.

As winter approached, we hired new staff. It was during this period that I met people from 'Border Paving', an outfit from the road construction industry. They worked in the summer and got laid off in the winter, so they would work jobs like this until road building started up again. I became friends with these people and they encouraged me to apply for a job at Border Paving.

While I was still working at Revelstoke, one of the yard staff, Bob, had an older brother called Ken. Ken became a truck driver and forklift operator at Revelstoke. He was about ten years older than me and we became friends. He advised me to quit Revelstoke and work for Border Paving, where he worked in the summer as a grader operator. The road building work was usually out of town, hours were long and work was hard.

Ken told me he would call me next spring and get me a job as a road builder and labourer. He liked that I could operate forklifts and drive trucks because there was a lot of equipment in road building, and Border Paving liked people with experience operating it. I was being paid $1.50 per hour at Revelstoke and the pay at Border Paving started at $8.00 per hour. I was very excited to find a job that paid this much money.

Due to their help, I was hired, and started my new well-paying career in road construction.

My First Girlfriend & Leaving Home

This would be my last Christmas home with Marj and my sisters. I was never home much, maybe a couple of days every two weeks, and I enjoyed the freedom. I partied a lot with people at Border Paving, and had gotten into drugs and drinking.

My first girlfriend and I met in the fall of 1978 when I was sixteen. When I saw her for the first time, I thought she was beautiful. We went to the same high school. I was in grade eleven, she was in grade ten, and we met through my middle sister, who had given us directions to a party she was going to.

Despite my awkwardness around girls, we managed to connect that evening. I soon discovered that she was kind and loving, soft-spoken, smart, and gentle, had a good sense of humour and to my surprise, she seemed to like me! She and her family would become a large part of my life, and remain so, even to this day. I am very close to them. I enjoyed visiting their house and did so often.

I knew that sooner rather than later, I would be moving out of Marj's house. I had been out of the house for the last two summers because of my road construction work, and Marj and Sweetums had gotten used to me not being home. If I did sleep at home, my girlfriend stayed in my room.

That summer, Marj told me she didn't like my girlfriend sleeping over, and that it had to stop. Marj thought I was too serious about her and should break it off. I was dumbfounded. I had found a beautiful, loving, happy girl from a family without drama. I loved them and they were a huge positive influence on me.

Finally we had a heated argument and I told her, "Fuck you. I am out of here."

During the night, I heard Marj sneak into my room and take my house keys. That meant I was out of the house for good. That morning, I loaded up whatever clothes I could carry. Marj and Sweetums yelled to me, "And stay out!"

MY FIRST APARTMENT

I found a one-bedroom apartment, furnished it, and began living on my own as of July 1st, 1978. I made it through the winter with money I made from stealing.

A Change of Forecast

When I moved out, or got thrown out - whichever way you look at it, I had to learn how to do my own laundry. When I had lived at home, my sisters always did the laundry. I would put my dirty clothes in a pile in front of the washing machine, and in a few hours, they were magically washed, dried and folded.

It was summer and I had been working in construction. I avoided washing them to the point where some of the smells on my clothes would be considered toxic by most people. My co-workers told me it was time to either wash my clothes or go and get new ones.

So finally, on one blistering hot day, I packed up all my clothes and anything else that could pass off as laundry, and left for the laundromat. The nearest one was in a small strip mall not far from where I lived. There was a drugstore there to buy detergent, and a 'Taco Time', so I had everything I needed in one place.

The asphalt that day was untouchable for bare feet - safe to say no one was expecting snow. I pulled up to the laundromat, grabbed my clothes and strolled inside. It took a few seconds for my eyes to adjust to the dim lighting. All the washing machines were neatly laid out in a long row along one side of the room. On the other side, in the same row, were the dryers. The air smelled of detergent and the heat and smell of drying clothes. There was a long table in the middle of the room, on which users would fold their clothes. At the end of the room, there were chairs for people waiting, to sit on.

A few young moms were laughing and talking in the corner. A couple was folding the last of their clothes, and another one sat in the waiting area. Perfect. I could use the machines without waiting.

I walked up to one and flipped open the lid, stuffed in my clothes and started to read the instructions. My load took up three washing machines. As I was reading, I thought to myself, "This is not that difficult. Any fool could do it."

I smiled to myself. This would just be one more thing to cross off my list of independent accomplishments. I walked over to the change machines and changed my dollars for quarters. With my pockets heavy, I walked out to the drug store and bought a large box of laundry soap and Bounce sheets for the dryer.

Returning to the machines, I poured a third of the detergent box into each of the three washers, put in the quarters and pushed the plunger with the coins in. I heard the machine gobble up the quarters, and water started pouring in to the tank. I turned around and saw two of the moms staring at me, watching everything I was doing. Satisfied that everything was in order, I slammed the lids down on all three washing machines and headed for the drugstore again.

I thumbed through Playboy and Penthouse before buying my usual Ellery Queen mystery magazine. I spent a good half hour in the drug store before thinking it was time to check on the washing machines. I paid for the magazine and strolled back to the laundromat.

Once inside, I stopped in my tracks, stunned. The entire area in front of my three machines was covered in soapsuds high enough to reach my waist. More was spewing out, like lava from a volcano. The suds were spilling out through the length of the entire room. I could hear the two young moms at the back, laughing hysterically. I broke into a sweat, completely stumped on how to clean this up.

A fool can do this? I asked myself. I grabbed my laundry basket from the folding-table and started scooping up the suds. I ran out to the parking lot and dumped them out. I ran back and forth frantically, scooping the suds, over and over.

The two moms were laughing so hard I thought they would pee themselves. Eventually, I managed to scoop up most of the suds on the floor.

The washing machines had thankfully finished their cycles, and new suds stopped pouring out. Looking outside, I could see the soapsuds – they took up four empty parking spots. They looked like the snow banks plows made when they cleaned up snowstorms.

I opened the washing machines and looked at the lumps of unused laundry soap that were stuck to all my things. It was a disaster. I pulled my soap-caked clothes from each washing machine and made a pile of them on the floor. I pulled all the leftover soap chunks and put them in the garbage. The two moms had stopped laughing and were folding their clothes on the table. I ignored them, deep in my own misery now as I tried to clean up the mess I had created.

I could hear the two moms talking about me. They must have known I could hear every word they said. As they gathered up their freshly laundered and folded clothes into their baskets, they made a point of walking by me. I looked up at them. One of them looked at me and then at the mess of soap and wet clothes on the floor. She turned back to me, smiling.

"I think you used too much soap!!"

They both broke into hysterical laughter. It continued as they passed through the parking lot, looking over their shoulders at the sudsy snow bank.

That was the day I changed the forecast.

Border Paving - Rick

In the spring of 1977, I had just turned sixteen when I began my career at Border. I started working with a crew that raised water valves, manholes and fire hydrants to the finished elevation before the paving began. This meant I was out of town as soon as I was hired. After that, I wouldn't be home for months at a time.

One day while at work, I was instructed to meet the surveyor and help him complete his layouts. His name was Rick Dale and he was supposed to be waiting for me. When I arrived, the only person I saw was a guy in a leather biker's vest. A grim reaper and sickle were embroidered on the back with 'Grim Reapers' written at the top. He had a goatee, long hair and piercing blue eyes. I could see tattoos on his arms and a large knife hanging from his belt, with another grim reaper embroidered on the sheath.

I went back into the office and asked the supervisor who exactly I was supposed to meet.

"The guy at the gas pumps. He's waiting for you."

My heart sank. He meant the biker! Quite frankly, he scared the shit out me. I thought that if I left with him he would kill me and leave my body in some field. I walked out to him and we got into his truck together. All the way out to the site, I hugged the truck door with my hand on the handle, ready to jump out at the first sign of danger.

Rick seemed to take great glee in scaring me. At first he didn't talk. He just stared at me and motioned at things in the truck he wanted taken out. After a few hours, he started talking. He wanted to know how old I was.

"Sixteen," I told him.

Throughout our week of working together, he asked me about my life. I shared some of what had happened to me and I explained a bit about my parents. He didn't say much about it. He simply told me life was not always fair.

Rick was a smart man. He had gone to the University of Japan, spoke Japanese, and knew karate. He was also the leader of the Grim Reapers. We became friends and I spent much of my summer with him, hanging out at his gang's clubhouse. I was never really part of the club - the guys simply considered me Rick's pet. Everyone knew how young I was.

I learned a lot of lessons from them. One of the members had gone to jail for sixteen months. He had a wife and two little kids. Rick told him before he went to jail that they would take care of his family for him, and they did. Every Saturday, Rick or someone from the gang would take a large box of food, diapers, toys, and clothes and drop them off. The men paid the rent, mowed the lawn, and took care of any car or house repairs.

After helping drop off supplies one day, I thought, here is a group that most people consider criminals, scum, no-goods, but I could not believe how tight they were as a family. I had seen how badly so-called good or normal families behaved. This group had the strongest family ties and sense of community I had seen until that point. They knew they only had each other to depend on and that made their bond stronger.

I almost wept when that thought hit me. I knew that if I ever needed help, they would be there, no questions asked. I liked Rick and his biker family. To me, they were good people. However, I also learned what happened when you lied to them.

There was a guy that wanted desperately to be part of the gang. He always hung out around the guys, and bought them booze and dope. Most of the group did not like him but would gladly drink and smoke his dope. He had none of the qualities Rick wanted in a member. He rode a shiny new Harley Davidson motorcycle and wore the clothes and boots to look the part.

But Rick wanted people in his club that were loyal, respectful, and honest with each other, kept their mouths shut, and knew that whatever was said amongst the gang stayed there. Silence was golden. Rick could not tolerate a big mouth and braggart, and that's what this guy was.

When Rick called a club meeting, the deal was that you went - no questions, no excuses. Your mother could be on her deathbed but you still showed up at the meetings. One day, Rick called a meeting and set it at a time when this guy definitely could not make it. Rick hinted that this would be an interesting meeting and that some things had to change. Everyone attended except the wannabe. There were no cell phones back then, and this wannabe had someone phone Rick to tell him he couldn't come.

His friend said it was because he was in the Innisfail Police Station, picked up for unpaid tickets. He said he had a relative coming to pay his bail and he would see Rick the next day. Rick was not unfamiliar with the jail. Rick called his bail bondsman and sent him to Innisfail to have the guy released. Rick knew he was not there but went through the motions anyway.

Later that day, the bondsman showed up and told Rick that he went to the jail, but the guy was not there, nor was there any record of him being held by the Innisfail RCMP. Rick nodded and smiled, handing the bondsman cash for his time. Rick called the guy to set up a meeting the next day. He told everyone in the gang to show up at the clubhouse as well.

The next afternoon, there were about fifteen to twenty guys at the clubhouse. The guy came riding up on his shiny new Harley, smiling a big smile. He waved to us and parked his bike, removed his helmet and gloves and walked over to Rick.

Rick looked him in the eyes and said, "So you were in lockup in Innisfail yesterday. I see you made it out okay."

"Yeah, they picked me up yesterday for unpaid traffic tickets. My brother-in-law came over and bailed me out."

Rick walked over to him and punched him in the solar plexus. He fell on the ground, writhing in pain and unable to breathe.

In a calm voice, Rick said, "You fucking liar, we sent a bondsman to get you out of jail and you weren't there."

As he spoke, Rick gave him a hard kick in the ribs, which made him writhe even more. Now, the rest of the guys started to circle so he couldn't escape. Rick beat him until he sobbed and begged for his life. He thought Rick was going to kill him.

"I am not going to kill you, you piece of shit, but you are going to be a lesson for everyone else. Let them all see what happens when someone lies."

The circle opened up, allowing the man to crawl towards his parked bike. Rick yelled at him, "The bike is mine. You can walk or crawl home. I don't give a shit, but the bike is mine so fuck off. If I ever see you again, trust me, it will be very painful."

We watched the guy struggle to his feet. He staggered down the road as everyone yelled at him.

I admired Rick's code of honour. I spent time with Rick and his friends throughout the next year and a half. He usually asked me to help him survey sites whenever I was available. I would drop by and have a few drinks and a smoke or two with the gang.

One day, the news announced that Rick had been killed on the job in Whitecourt, Alberta. He had bent down to adjust grade stakes on a new road Border Paving was building, when a van struck him. The road lane was closed for construction. The paving company told us the driver had been waving to a friend who was working on the road. He didn't see Rick bent down, as he veered towards the lane under construction, and struck Rick with his van.

I felt a deep loss that day. Rick was one of the first people I opened up to. He never judged me or said anything disagreeable to me. I had a kinship with Rick, although to the outside world, we had a strange and unlikely friendship.

Rick's funeral was very large, drawing in approximately five hundred bikers. They organized a riding procession for him with riders from all over the world. Rick had travelled extensively and knew a lot people. People from Red Deer and the surrounding area also attended. I remember my irritation with the RCMP's conduct.

Fearful of such a large biker gathering, they stopped and searched every biker in the procession. The riders were there to show respect for one of their own, not to stir up trouble. I admired the bikers' civility towards the RCMP in honour of Rick. Each biker went through a search and the RCMP found nothing, not even a traffic ticket.

The bikers never agitated the RCMP in any way. Finally they let all the bikers complete their ride in Rick's memory. About a week later, I dropped by the clubhouse and was greeted by a gang member named 'Animal'. No one else came out to greet me.

He said, "Greg we need to talk."

I felt something harden in the pit of my stomach.

"I know you and Rick had a close friendship and we respect that. But you were Rick's pet project and we left that alone. Now that Rick is gone, so are you. Rick had talked with us about you. We all agreed that you do not belong here, and there would be a day when this would come. You are out, gone, just like Rick. This is how it's going to work. You do not acknowledge us, wave to us, talk to us. You do not come to see us, ever. If you break these rules, we will kick the shit out of you each and every time."

I knew it was hard for Animal to tell me that. I had formed friendships with many people in the group, including him, but I knew they would do what he said to me. It was for the best. I turned around, got in my car and drove away, never looking back.

Master of My Abode

I continued living on my own for the next few years while going to high school. One week, I arrived at my Grade 11 English class after missing three classes, to find the English teacher wanting a note from my mother.

"I no longer live at home." I told her. "Here is my phone number at my new apartment. If you need me you can call me there. If I don't answer, I'm out. If you want a note, I will write one now for you."

She reported this to the principal right away, who called me to his office. When I arrived, there was a school counsellor sitting beside him.

"Why did you leave home?" the school counsellor asked.

"I couldn't get along with my mother and her live-in boyfriend."

"Have you or your family members been abused by him?" she asked.

"Not to my knowledge. They wanted me out and took my house keys. Honestly, I had had enough of both my parents and the boyfriends. At this point, it's just easier to live alone."

"Greg, you're still under eighteen. This is an interesting situation – you need to make money but still stay in high school. I imagine it must be hard to pay your own bills and work enough hours. I will find out if you are eligible for any help from the government."

About two months later, I was called to the office again. This time, the counsellor introduced me to the government social services caseworker. I wish I could remember her name because she was an amazing person. She asked me where I lived and I told her it was nearby. To my surprise, she said "How about I follow you over to your apartment right now?"

Intrigued, I decided to play along and showed her the way. She came inside to inspect my living conditions. All the furniture was brand new and I had everything I needed, even a vacuum cleaner. She walked around the apartment and noted my drug box and a pipe on the coffee table

Yes, my drug box. I had different types of drugs in there, and all of them could get me into serious trouble with the police. Living on my own and hanging out with the people I did, I was exposed to a lot of different types of drugs. I had tried and used many different drugs; pot, coke, acid, MDA, clinical speed, uppers, magic mushrooms and some I'm not sure what they were. Some drugs I liked to do, some I tried and didn't like the result of what it did to me. I liked alcohol, pot, speed, coke and MDA. I didn't care for acid or mushrooms. I did not like needles so I never injected myself with anything. The caseworker had a good point; I needed to be more discreet.

There were Penthouse and Playboy magazines out in full view, and there were empty beer cans stacked in the hall closet. There was beer in the fridge. She sat down in my kitchen chair.

"I want to hear your story. I need to know why a sixteen year-old would want to live on his own, two years before graduation."

Up until that moment, I had been acting cocky and giving her an 'I don't care' attitude, but she stopped me in my tracks. I looked at her and sat down at the kitchen table across from her. I cleared my throat. "What do you want to know?"

"I have a few hours. You can start at the beginning."

She pulled out her notebook to write everything down. Within a couple of hours, I had told her my history of abuse and leaving home.

"Why do you want to finish high school? You could quit and work full-time."

"No one in our family ever finished high school. I want to be the first."

She told me there would be no help from the government. All the education programs were for people over eighteen going back to school, not for someone that was sixteen and still trying to finish it. One option was to make me a ward of the government because of my age. I would be put in a foster home and cared for until graduation. I could also go to a government facility for fostering and education. That meant I'd be sent to juvenile hall without ever being charged for a crime.

"I won't leave what I have worked so hard to set up. I'm happy here."

"I'll file a report claiming myself as your sponsor," she said. "You will be living on your own under my supervision."

"What does that mean. Are you becoming my mother? No thanks, just gave one up."

She laughed. "No, not your mother. Just someone to check up on you. The government will pay you three hundred and fifty dollars a month for your living expenses. You give me an extra key, and I will come by every second Friday of the month to inspect your living conditions. I will come by until you graduate. But you have to keep everything clean – cleaner than it is now."

She surveyed the apartment. "That means the drug box, pipe, skin magazines, empty beer cans, and any alcohol in the fridge need to be out of sight. I may have to bring someone from my office to check your place with me so they can make sure I'm doing my job.

"You are underage, and a lot of these things you're doing are illegal. I realize you will probably continue doing them even if I tell you not to, so just be smart about it if you want to continue receiving help. I think it's better for you to live here than in foster care or juvi hall – just don't mess this up."

"If someone from the office makes a spot inspection or if a cop gets suspicious and follows you here, you have to at least be discreet. In addition, you will attend school on a regular basis and receive passing marks. You *must* work towards your high school diploma for the money to continue."

I took her advice. My apartment was always impeccable and always passed inspection when she stopped by every other Friday. For the first six months, I knew she came by regularly since she would leave me a note saying everything looked good.

The cheques came to my mailbox every month. At the beginning of grade twelve, she stopped coming by, but the cheques continued. The money the government gave me only covered my rent, and I had to come up with money for utilities, food and entertainment. I had savings left over from my job with Border Paving but I needed monthly money coming in. I didn't want to spend all my savings before school ended.

School ended in late June, which meant I could only get two months of full-time work in the whole year. I had to find other ways to make money.

I began stealing bikes and other items I could throw in the back of my truck. I would let people know that if they wanted a certain bike, a barbeque or something else, I could get it for them. They would name a pickup location and I delivered. I had a set price for each item and my clients paid me cash upon delivery.

Once an order was placed, I drove through town looking for the best places to steal what I needed.

I scanned the houses for dogs, fences, gates and parking availability. I usually stole 10-speed bikes, barbeques, tires, and rims. I never went into the house, only the yard and garage. I always stole at night. At first, my heart would pound so loud I thought people would hear it and find me. Eventually, my fear subsided.

Stealing was remarkably easy. I stole a 10-speed bike from the back door of a house while the family sat with their backs to the window, watching TV. I stayed hidden until the commercials were over. I wanted to make sure no one would be going to the fridge or bathroom. Once the TV show came back on, I waited a few more minutes, slid up to the back door and grabbed the bike. I quickly wheeled it to the back alley where my truck, still running, was waiting for me. I threw the bike into the back, quietly opened the door and drove silently down the alley. When I reached the street, I drove away as fast the speed limit allowed.

To avoid suspicion, I sold the items right away, setting up the exchange with the buyer as soon as possible.

I did this for two years to put myself through high school. I had many customers, and some were repeats. Some of my clients surprised me. They weren't people you would expect to find buying stolen goods.

Could I have made my living honestly? I could have gotten a part-time job for $3.00 per hour. I would have had to work every day after school and on weekends. Still I wouldn't have had enough to pay my bills.

However, I did have one part-time job in the winter when I was seventeen.

My middle sister got a job working at the nicest hotel in Red Deer. It was a hot spot, with restaurants, bars, and banquet rooms. She knew how I was making my extra money and wanted me to cut down. She told me I should apply to the hotel because they were looking for bar staff.

"But I'm only seventeen. What if they ask for ID?"

"I'll tell the staff you're eighteen and you're looking for a bartending job."

She set up the interview. The bar manager never even asked for ID. They were swamped and needed more bartenders right away. I said I could work weekends but not during the week when I was going to school. He knew I was going to high school and assumed that I had just turned eighteen. I backdated my date of birth by one year on my application form, signed my name, and was promptly hired.

I worked all types of bartending gigs, weddings, banquets, the lounge and the party rock and roll bar. I didn't enjoy the party bar. It was stressful and the drink orders never stopped coming.

On some nights, there were fights among the patrons. The serving girls were overwhelmed by the number of orders and the rowdy behavior, and I felt bad for them as they were on the front lines.

I learned to recognize the three types of drunks: lovers, criers, and fighters. When I began the job, the bar manager gave me the 'thou shall not' rules for bartending. One of these rules was the bartender never leaves the bar to help out in a fight.

He told me the bouncers would take care of anything on the other side of the bar, and the bartenders would take care of their side. He pointed to fish bats lying on a low shelf under the bar. If any hands, fingers or people came on my side of the bar, I was to hit them with the fish bat.

He explained that patrons would sometimes stage a fight to get the whole bar involved. When the bartenders left the bar to help, thieves would break into the cash register and steal the liquor. I never had to hit anyone during my bartending but the fighting made the job stressful.

I talked to the RCMP when they came in to do spot checks for underage drinkers. I would laugh to myself when I saw a minor slip into the bathroom when the cops walked in, and I'd tip the cops off. One would go in and a few minutes later come out holding the minor by the back of his collar. They were taken outside to the cop car to be issued a ticket and fined.

I discovered many years later that the bar could have gotten into serious trouble, possibly even shut down for having a minor serving liquor.

Eventually, I got tired of going to bed when the sun rose and waking up at sunset. I often described my job as working at the vampire club. Ironically, I quit bartending just after I turned eighteen. Stealing was for me; I made better money, faster and easier.

Changing My Life

During the last years of high school, I became very close to my girlfriend's family, spending most of my time at their farm just outside Red Deer. I never told them what I was doing, since I wanted to keep my illegal activity to myself.

I became good friends with her two brothers, and came to love her mom and dad. I called her mother, 'Mom'.

They helped me through some difficult times, and they helped me become who I am today. They were there for me, from the moment I first met them at sixteen years old, to this very day.

My girlfriend's dad taught me how to barter and not let myself be taken advantage of, financially. He taught me a strong work ethic, helped me develop my sense of humour, and taught me to be self-reliant. He was always gentle, though he was tough when he had to be. Her mom loved me as her own son. She had a great sense of humour, and could cook up a storm in the kitchen. They loved their kids and they loved each other. They were the family I never had.

My girlfriend and I went out for four years, and had some good times. She knew my Granny, and they liked each other. We often went to Granny's and stayed for a few days. I really enjoyed our time at Granny's because I did not drink, smoke or do any drugs. She connected with my grandmother and she was at my side during Granny's funeral. Granny had always told me that she was good for me. She thought I ought to settle down with her as my wife, and start behaving myself.

When I graduated from high school, her parents were in the audience watching me receive my high school diploma. I felt so proud that someone loved and cared about what I had accomplished.

After graduation, I continued to work for Border Paving. Being a seasonal job, I did road construction in the summer and worked on oilrigs and pipelines in the winter. Once in 1982, while working on an oil service rig on a gas well, there was not enough fluid pumped down the well to hold down the natural gas pressure. As we were putting the pipe back down into the gas well, after having laid down ten or twelve lengths of a twenty-foot pipe, we heard a hissing sound like a boiling kettle. The whistling became louder and louder until it sounded like a steam train.

I looked to the guy beside me; all I saw was his feet as he jumped over the rig's platform railing to get off the rig we were on. The rest of the crew ran from the rig platform as fast as they could go. I jumped over the railing and landed on the ground on my knees. I looked up at the rig and saw the one hundred and twenty feet of pipe we had put down the hole, fly into the air like a stream of black spaghetti! The pipe twisted and bent as it spewed out of the well. Each twenty-foot length of pipe weighed two to three hundred pounds or more and each connected together; they weighed more than a ton.

As I watched them fly through air, my brain screamed, it's going to come down and if it hits you, you'll die.

The adrenaline kicked in and I started to crawl away. Then, I got to my feet and ran to the edge of the field. There, I watched the pipe land on top of the rig, crushing and smashing everything it hit.

After the pipe finished falling, the driller went to the Blow Out Prevention (BOP) shed and closed off the well. He called for a truck to come and pump more fluid down the hole, and arranged for the damaged rig to be removed. He called in a rig team working nearby to help us clean everything up. The next morning, we were back on the same well site with a different rig and completed the job.

A few months later, we were to go to the Lodge Pole area to work on gas wells, about thirty kilometres from Drayton Valley. Many of the gas wells in this area contained a deadly gas, hydrogen sulphide - H2S. It would render you unconscious in a minute or less. Death was within four minutes. Our rig was scheduled to work in this area for the next six months. On our way to Drayton Valley, our rig broke down and required major engine repairs. One rig in the company was finishing their scheduled work and they were sent to replace us.

When their rig was set up over the gas well and it was opened, the entire crew was overcome by hydrogen sulphide, and two workers died. There was so much concentrated gas being released that it spread quickly through the area, killing everything in its path: birds, wild animals, cattle, and horses. The area was isolated so, other than the crewmembers, no other people were affected. The oil company could not turn off the well, which continued to spew two hundred and eighty thousand tons of H2S gas over sixty-seven days.

People as far as Winnipeg, Manitoba, over fifteen hundred kilometres away, could smell the gas. The famous oil firefighter Red Adair was called in to close it off.

My job meant that I was often away, and this was hard on my girlfriend and our relationship. When I was home, I led the party life, drinking and doing drugs. I often came to take her out for the evening and instead would end up going out to drink with her older brother and his friends. Towards the end of our relationship, I was also cheating on her. She was a saint on earth to put up with me.

Eventually, she enrolled in a two-year computer program in Edmonton at the Northern Alberta Institute of Technology (NAIT). During the first year she lived in Edmonton, she met someone in her program and they began dating.

I remember the Saturday she came to see me in Red Deer. We went to a park, and she told me she had met someone else and that we were finished. I had been thinking about our time together and was planning my future with her in it. I enjoyed being with her and had planned to propose to her that summer. I have never blamed her for anything during our time together and I take full responsibility for us falling apart. I felt as if I had betrayed all that she and her family had done for me.

I still feel guilty about how hurt she was when she found out I had cheated. She hadn't known at the time. I hope that she can forgive me one day. After she broke up with me, I was depressed and threw myself into drinking, drugs and partying. I knew I had deserved what had happened.

Later that year, after drinking at a bar, I was following some friends to their place. I ran a yellow light and got pulled over by the RCMP, where I promptly failed a breathalyzer test, and was arrested for drunk driving. The officers put me in the back of their car and had my car towed. They took me to the police station and put me in the drunk tank for the night. As I was sobering up, I asked the cop on duty if I could walk home, since I only lived five blocks away. I was polite and he had a brother-in-law working at Border Paving, so he cut me a break. He let me leave once I signed the paperwork for the arrest.

My court date was scheduled two months later. For this meeting, I could decide if I wanted a lawyer to represent me and dispute the charges. I decided I deserved what I got for all the times I had driven drunk without consequences. I would not fight the charge, and I would represent myself.

I asked the prosecutor if I could keep my license until November 15th, after which I would plead guilty and hand it over. The prosecutor said he would look into it and give me an answer on my court date.

I appeared before the judge around the middle of May. The prosecutor had called around to check up on my background. He had also called Border Paving about my request, and Border said I was a good worker. They needed me until the work season ended and it would be helpful if the court would let me keep my license. The prosecutor then said he would not oppose my request, and to let him do the talking when the judge asked for my plea.

I was nervous in the courtroom. There is a reason the judge's podium is so high. He can look down on you and make you feel so very small.

"Mr. Reid, how do you plead to the charge of driving with your blood alcohol level exceeding the legal limit of 0.08?"

I looked over at the prosecutor, who stepped forward, head bowed.

"Your honour, Mr. Reid came to me after he was arrested for drunk driving and explained that he needs to keep his license to remain employed. He would like to reconvene this court appearance on November 15 this year. On that date, Mr. Reid has promised he will plead guilty and surrender his license to the court. We have contacted his employer and done a criminal background check and we, the Crown Council, do not object to this request."

The prosecutor bowed again, turned sharply and went back to his table.

The judge looked down at me. "Upon this recommendation, I will allow you to keep your license. You must know this is a gift - you should be turning over your license. If you show up in front of me or any other judge again for the same offence before your rescheduled court appearance, I won't be very happy, and you will receive the maximum penalty."

He turned to the bailiff taking notes. "Let the record show that this docket has been rescheduled for November, 15 this year."

He looked at me. "Remember what I said, Mr. Reid. This is a gift from the court. Do not disappoint us. This case is adjourned. You may now leave."

I thanked the prosecutor for his help, and he too, told me not to disappoint him for his favour. I told him I understood and thanked him again. I decided right then that I was not going to be drinking and driving anytime soon.

After that, I still drank, but I didn't drive. That put a damper on my partying since we all drove drunk from bars to parties and from parties to bars. I became the designated driver and I began to see what went on when everyone else was drunk. It was not pretty.

One weekend, I found myself at a rugby party. I spotted my ex-girlfriend's brother in the crowd. I could tell he had already had a few too many. I wandered around, listening to drunks tell their stories, when I noticed a fight breaking out between some of the rugby players and my girlfriend's brother and his friends. He was totally out of it. He was frothing at the mouth and very belligerent.

The rugby players were getting worked up and wanted to beat him up. His friends got scared and ran away, leaving him there on his own.

Things were going from bad to dangerous. I ran over and stood between the rugby players and my girlfriend's brother, and told the rugby players that if they beat on him, he might die. I told them I knew this guy, and that I would get him out of there. They needed to leave him alone.

They called me names and threatened to pound on me too but I told them I would call the police and give every one of their names. This was enough to make them back off.

I tried to take him to the hospital, as I was worried about alcohol poisoning, but he became violent, so I took him home to his brother.

We spent the night walking him around and keeping him awake so he did not lose consciousness. After a long night, I finally arrived at my apartment. I thought about my father's drinking and how it affected our lives, my girlfriend breaking up with me, my impaired driving charge. Seeing her brother that way was the final act in my spiraling life

I was going to stop drinking.

Martial Arts

While I worked in construction, the guys and I would often play-wrestle and fool around. They would often overpower me and pin me to the ground. I didn't like feeling that helpless. It made me remember the childhood beatings.

I started thinking about Tae Kwon Do. I needed discipline in my life and I was a big fan of the Bruce Lee movies, so I thought it would be cool to learn to defend myself. Deep down, I knew I wanted to beat someone up, if the opportunity arose. So, one evening that summer, I went down to the local Tae Kwon Do club and told the trainer I wanted to take classes.

As it turned out, one of the instructors was an old boyfriend of my middle sister's. When I last saw him, he had been dealing with drug addiction, and I lost contact with him after he and my sister broke up.

When I walked into the club, I was taken aback. He was in incredible shape. He was almost a black belt, with one more test to take. It was impressive.

Doug told me I could take a couple of classes for free to see if I liked it. He was an assistant instructor, who filled in for the regular instructor during the week or gave extra lessons if the class wanted it.

I could barely walk the day after my first class. Although I was strong enough for shoveling, digging and lifting heavy equipment, I had never stretched a day in my life! I never lifted my feet higher than I'd need to, to climb a stair.

Doug was a brutal instructor. He made us do workouts that bordered on cruelty. He told us he was going to make us flexible. This, he said, was the key to martial arts. He was not kidding. That was all we seemed to do - work out and stretch.

Tae means to kick, Kwon means to punch, and Do means to complete the action or simply 'Do'. That is what we did, class after class, week after week, month after month.

The head black belt of the club was Geoff Low, who was from China, and had learned Wing Chung growing up. We asked him why he had moved to Canada. He told us if he hadn't left China, he would have gone to prison for life. Geoff told me that he had been running with the wrong crowd and his name was listed with an order for arrest. His father had a friend in the police force and when he saw Geoff's name, he warned Geoff's father. Geoff had a day or two to pack up and leave the country. He packed a few meager belongings and set off for Canada. He came as a landed immigrant, and decided to take advantage of our education system. He received scholarships and became a psychologist.

Geoff and I became good friends. With his teaching, I lived and breathed martial arts. In time, I understood how to fight, and I too became quite good. My childhood of abuse left me with an advantage – I had a high tolerance for pain. That, together with my new skill, made me a strong opponent. I fought as a demon possessed. During my training, Geoff would tell me I had a deadly genie bottled up inside, and one day, it would come out. He said I fought like I didn't care about anything or anyone, and I seemed not to be afraid of serious injury or death - I focused only on beating my opponent. Sometimes, I pretended my opponents were Allen or Marj, and unleashed all my emotions.

In learning to fight, I discovered my own power, and my fear subsided. My personality went from quiet and calm to aggressive and angry. I was able to beat most all of the opponents I fought and I found I enjoyed it. I beat up many people, and I want to offer my apologies. I only fought this way with the higher belts and students who were supposed to be better than me. I never hurt or harmed the younger students or students who were weaker than me. I wanted a piece of the better students, the higher belts, the instructors; only the very best.

I was mean, I had a high tolerance for pain, I never backed down, and it made me feel good to beat other people up, one after another. Those I didn't beat, I still hurt them. If they won, I made sure I hurt them in the process.

While I was losing, I would say to myself, "I may lose this fight...but I will take a piece of you with me so you will never forget this fight. We'll see if you'll want to fight me again."

Some of my opponents, many of those who were black belts, would refuse to fight me again.

The Bully

Many years later living in BC, in the lower mainland, I started with a karate club in Langley. It was your run-of-the-mill martial art studio. The instructor was very mellow and had a gentle leadership style, which is okay if you're running a library.

A large part of martial arts is discipline. Most studios require the instructor to be firm with their students when they get out of line. Order is of utmost importance.

I had been with the club for about three months and was starting to figure out what everyone's skill level was. Amongst the students, there was this guy who was just one level below a black belt. He was the senior belt of the club, just under the instructor. His next step was the black belt test, the holy grail of martial arts. He really thought he was something, always bragging about how he beat some guy up. He had stories upon stories. He was a real piece of work. He took advantage of sparring time at the club to hurt others, too.

Sparring was an essential part of our classes. We wore arm and leg pads, and rotated until everyone had sparred with everyone else. Sparring was a chance to practice the skills we learned – it basically means fighting another partner, only to practice. It works well when two students have the same belts, strength and skill. They can spar together to better develop their fighting skills. The coach can instruct them on how best to do this. Or, if one is stronger, he can help train the weaker student to improve. This is supposed to be a mutually beneficial part of martial arts. When students start to beat up on those younger and weaker, the instructor is to step in and set the situation straight.

This bully liked to rough up younger students during these sessions. With older and stronger students, he took cheap shots, made low kicks and 'accidentally' punched their faces.

When I first started, I managed to evade his cheap-shot kicks and punches. I noticed that after he would fail to get the best of me, he would be even more aggressive with his next sparring partner.

After a couple of months of watching this guy's behaviour, I was starting to get pissed off. I talked to the instructor about it and he said he hadn't noticed anything wrong, and none of the other students had ever complained. He even said the guy helped the other students improve, including myself, and I should be proud of him.

I left the dojo flabbergasted. The whole philosophy behind martial arts was acting in the way of the peaceful warrior and leading by example. This place was a dud, I thought to myself.

After the instructor's response, my heart was not really in the club anymore. During my next sparring match, I wasn't concentrating and fought sloppily. I was fighting the bully, and he gave me a nasty cheap shot. I wasn't quick enough, and suddenly, the wind was knocked out of me. As I lay there trying to catch my breath, he started taunting me and being a real asshole. The round was over and we switched partners. I started planning my revenge.

The next week, I was ready for him. I took it easy with the warm-up exercises and held back during the kicking and punching drills. I was saving all my strength and stamina for when he and I would spar. Finally, the instructor told us to gear up and get in position for sparring. I could hardly wait - I really was looking forward to it.

After a couple of rotations, the bully and I were facing each other. I gave no sign that this match would be any different from the others. He was in for a surprise. As he punched and kicked at me, I blocked and countered, waiting for his cheap shot. As I knew he would, he tried to give a low kick to my groin, which I blocked. Then, I kicked him as hard I could in the ribs. I heard him grunt with pain, and before he could turn, with all my power I kicked the same spot again. I heard a cracking sound at the second kick.

As he fell to the ground clutching his side, I jumped on top of him and started punching him in the face. It took a few seconds for the rest of the class to notice what was going on between us. He was starting to cry out for help while I punched him in the head. He couldn't protect himself very well since he didn't want to take his arm off his damaged ribs, so he just left his head unprotected.

Finally, the instructor noticed what was going on and ran over to us. He grabbed me from behind and pulled me off. I don't know if I would have stopped beating him if the instructor hadn't stepped in.

He yelled, "What is going on here?"

I broke free and said, "This asshole tried to kick me in the balls while we were sparring, so I kicked him back."

My sparring buddy could barely get up. The instructor helped him to get to the changing room. When our instructor came back, he told me he wanted me out of the club immediately. He asked me to take all my gear and leave, never to come back. I didn't care. I knew I was going to be kicked out when I fought him. More than anything, I wanted to teach this asshole a lesson in front of the other students. They deserved to see him take a beating for all he did to them.

Later on, I received a phone call from the instructor telling me the guy had two broken ribs and would not be going to class for eight weeks. The guy also wanted to charge me with assault, but he couldn't. We all signed a waiver when we began training that said no one was liable if someone got hurt in the dojo while practicing martial arts. I had counted on that.

I felt so good when it was over. I knew I had an anger problem because I enjoyed the whole thing. I enjoyed feeling his ribs break. You know when you break someone's ribs because you can feel it happening. I knew I was hurting him, and I didn't care, it felt so damn good.

For all the years I was abused, beat up, teased, bullied and pushed around, I finally felt I like had some power over my life for once. Deep down, I felt I was like him, but at that point it didn't matter and I didn't care. I finally felt like the good guy and I deserved that feeling. Nothing and no one was going to take it away from me – myself included.

Now, I had to find another martial art studio. I never told anyone the real reason I left the karate club. I just said I wanted a break.

For the next 20 years I trained with weapons and learned different styles of combat techniques. I became a martial arts and weapons expert. I knew in my heart there was no one out there that could beat me because I was willing to fight to the death, if needed.

No one I fought could match my ferocity, and for that I thank my parents. I almost died at their hands. I was not scared of death – I remembered my experience on the driveway. When that is the state of a fighter's mind, it is a dangerous thing.

Unfortunately, martial arts got me in touch with an ugly side of myself. Perhaps it was inevitable. Nevertheless, the anger I unleashed would control me for the next part of my life. I carried the fighting instinct I honed in martial arts into my family and work life, just what they tell you not to do. The good news? I could defend myself. The bad news? I turned into a mean, angry, vicious, bullying person that most people would be unable and unwilling to deal with.

My new sense of power would become my downfall. The deadly genie was coming out of the bottle, just as Geoff had predicted.

This was the start of my breakdown, but it would develop for over twenty-seven years before it finally hit me.

As singer Boz Scaggs sings, "There's a Breakdown Dead Ahead".

It wasn't IF, it was WHEN.

Author's Note

I have discovered, there are two levels to heal all trauma. The first level is physical, which is forgiveness. This is essential to start the healing process of the pain of trauma. It wasn't going to be easy, but I was determined to heal myself.

Follow my journey in book two, due out in 2014. A sneak preview is provided in the next few pages.

My Contact Info:

Email: greg@greglreid.ca
Website: http://greglreid.ca

Let's Connect on Social Media:

Facebook: facebook.com/Greg-L-Reid
Twitter: https://twitter.com/Greg_L_Reid
LinkedIn: ca.linkedin.com/in/greglreid/
Google Plus: https://plus.google.com/u/0/110620402691809250108
Pinterest: http://pinterest.com/greglreid/

GREG L. REID

Sierra

Excerpt From Book Two

Sierra – Excerpt From Book Two

Ah, the normal weather of the Okanagan - hot as hell all day and then a nasty electrical storm with big winds and hard rain at night.

I was in George's camper trailer, directly in front of the boat docks, watching the storm blow in. After dinner, the campground owner warned us that if we had boats, Sea-Doos, awnings, anything that could blow away or get damaged, to deal with it now. Kalamalka Lake was going to get very choppy, and hail was a possibility. Our family had just bought a new Sea-Doo, and the approaching storm made me ever watchful on my new water toy. George was concerned about his boat.

Just a week earlier, he had called, "Heinrich, do you have Saturday's Vancouver Sun?" He always called me Heinrich, as he was German.

"Heinrich, Sea-Doo is having a blow out and there are some good deals. I know you wanted to buy a lake toy. There's a dealer less than five minutes from you. Why don't you go up and check a Sea-Doo out. "

"Yeah, George, I have the Sun out now. Yeah, I see the ad. It looks good. I'll drive up and see them. Thanks for the tip. I'll let you know what happens. Smell you later."

An hour later, I had purchased my brand new Sea-doo, and was ready for the lake.

There was a large group of us at the Tween Lake Campground. The families had kids the same age, and they all enjoyed boating, wakeboarding and camping. The adults enjoyed drinking too. Many had had permanent campsites here for years. It was a good place to get away from the Coast.

When I brought home the new toy, everyone in the family came out of the house to ohhh and ahhh. It was bitching; a deep rich burgundy red with metal flake and sparkling pearl accents that sparkled and gleamed in the sunlight. Nice and sleek, with a back deck to get in and off of, it carried three passengers. It had an electronic display console, and the best part – A 115hp engine. With one person on it, you could reach speeds of 120 kph. This thing was fucking fast, a motorcycle on a lake, and it was dangerous. Our group was very safety conscious and everyone, including the kids, knew the rules. If anyone of them screwed up, they would be banned from using any watercraft.

'Well, Heinrich, another shot of tequila?"

"Well, there's fuck else I can do, other than watch my brand new Sea-Doo get smashed up."

We drank more tequila shots, while watching our boats and jet skis get tossed up, down and sideways. I vaguely remember going out with George and Brad, trying to wrestle down one of the Sea-Doos that had broken loose.

The storm was now in full force and the strong wind made it hard to breath. The rain had turned to hail, and any bare skin was turning red. It was fucking brutal. We barely managed to get the Sea-Doo under control and up on the beach. After tying it down, we all went back to George's trailer, soaked to the skin, bruised, battered and miserable. After a few more hours of drinking, I stood outside on the beach, looked up into the pounding hail and howling wind and yelled.

"You call this a storm?"

"This is not a storm! "

"I've had and seen fucking worse."

"Is this all ya fucking got?"

Finally, not able to take anymore of the pelting hail, I surrendered and staggered back to the trailer.

"What, you give up?" someone called from inside.

"What, you a fucking sissy?"

"Pussy."

"Didn't you say you've had worse?"

I caught sight of myself in the mirror. I looked like a drowned rat, hair matted to my scalp, red marks all over my body from the pounding hail. My expression sent everyone into hysterical laughter.

"Fuck all of ya!" I yelled to them. More laughter.

"Tequila!" I yelled. "More tequila!"

Hours later someone managed to help me stagger from George's trailer to our camper. I slipped into blackness.

Later, I heard my wife calling my name. I slowly awakened. It was stifling, my head was pounding, and my mouth parched and desert-sand dry. It felt like some animal had crawled in there and died. My whole body hurt from head to toe. I could see and feel the bruises on my arms and legs. I felt like I had been beaten up inside and out. Fuck did I feel like shit.

"You've slept for hours. It's late in the day." She said this quietly, knowing I was severely hung-over.

"Why are you wearing Brad's shorts? Never mind, I don't want to know. Get up and join us. We're all at Woods Lake beach for the day. I know you're hung-over but I don't care, get motivated. Join the world." She closed the door of the camper behind her as she left.

I moaned. I didn't want to get up. I wanted to be left in fucking peace and quiet to die. I lay there, listening to the singing, chirping birds in the trees around the camper. Slowly, sounds of kids yelling and laughing filtered in. Finally I could hear, softly and far away, in the background, peoples' voices in different conversations. Fuck me, I hurt. I rolled my legs over the edge of the bed, swung myself into a sitting position and placed my head in my hands, gently rocking it back and forth.

Why was I wearing Brad's shorts? They were three sizes too big, and how they stayed on was a mystery. Well, I'd clear up that question when I saw him, I thought, wondering if he was as hungover as I was. I pulled myself upright, grabbed my shaving kit, towel and shorts that would fit, and headed for the bathroom and shower building. It was empty at this late hour. I looked at myself in the mirror: red bloodshot bleary eyes, three days of beard stubble and hair that looked like a witch's wig. I looked like I had been run over by a car.

Yeah, I could clean myself up a bit. After a long hot shower, a clean smooth shave, and a toothbrush to remove the dead animal from my mouth, I felt much better. Not great, but better. I packed everything back up and walked back to the camper. I opened the fridge, pulled out and guzzled three bottles of water with aspirin and Gravol, and ate some cheese and crackers. Then I grabbed my lawn chair and headed over to the beach to join the rest of the group.

As I walked across the road, I could see the train bridge that crossed the canal and joined Kalamalka Lake with Woods Lake. It was narrow and shallow, and only one boat at a time could use it to move from one lake to the other. It was always busy with boats lined up on each side waiting their turn to go through but today it was busier than usual. I walked down the slope, looking for the group.

"So, how you feeling?" they snickered, as I plunked my lawn chair down beside them.

"Well, I look better on the outside than I do on the inside," I complained.

They laughed heartily.

I settled into my chair, opened another bottle of water and scanned the lake. Sea-Doos, boats and pulling tubes, wake boarders, water skiers and boats raced around. There was a long line up of boats and Sea-Doos waiting to go through the canal.

Lots of kids were swimming, splashing and enjoying the lake on such a hot day. The beach was completely packed with sunbathers and beach goers. I settled back in my chair, hoping I could catch some uninterrupted sleep.

As I dozed, out of the corner of my left eye I noticed a jet ski that had just come through the canal. A dad with a little girl riding in front raced along in front of the beach. I could hear her laughing and encouraging him to go faster. It was about 4:30pm and the sun had just set below hills to the west. From the surface of the lake to sloping beach, highway and hillside were now different tones of grey. It was difficult to make out specific detail; it all blended together.

A low-slung speedboat now left the beach area and headed south onto Woods Lake directly into the path of the speeding Jet Ski. I leaned out of my chair to focus on the Jet Ski, trying to determine if it was slowing down or changing course. My heart started to race. Neither the Jet Ski or speedboat was aware of each other; the Jet Ski was not slowing down or changing course.

I panicked. Before I could yell, the Jet Ski slammed full force into the side of the speedboat. Bodies flew into the air. I jumped out of my chair, hearing the yells and screams of people on the beach.

At the accident scene, there were people thrashing about, and a body lying in the water. I had taken first aid training during my years in construction, and I knew we had to get the injured to shore, as the land-based emergency people and equipment could not get out to the accident scene.

"Greg!" I yelled. Greg, who was part of our group, had his boat moored in front.

"Greg! Start your fucking boat now, we need to get to those people! Gilles, I'm going to need your help to pull people out of the water and get them to shore, I need you in the boat now!"

Greg fumbled with the key. At first, the boat wouldn't start.

"Greg, start the fucking boat!" I yelled at him. "Do whatever it takes to start this fucking thing, now!"

Greg ignored me, as he seemed to be willing the boat to start. Greg looked scared. Finally the engine coughed to life.

As we pulled away from shore, Heather, from our group, yelled to us, "I'm a nurse, I can help, take me with you."

She came to the back of the boat to climb in, as the propeller spun. She didn't seem to notice this danger but I did. I leaned over the back end of the boat and grabbed her arm before she could get close to the prop. With all my strength I pulled her up into the boat. Later Heather told me later my strength was so incredible, she felt as if she was flying through the air. She felt for a second that I would dislocate or break her arm.

I turned to the beach and screamed at the top of my lungs, "CALL 911! CALL FUCKING 911! NOW!"

GREG L. REID